*A Survival Guide for Choosing
Evolution Over Self-Destruction*

SUBVERSIVE
ACTS OF
HUMANITY

KEN BRENIMAN

Subversive Acts of Humanity:

A Survival Guide for Choosing Evolution Over Self-Destruction

Copyright © 2025, Ken Breniman

Published by:

Mindfully Mortal Publications

A Note on Sharing

This book is meant to be shared, adapted, and built upon. Every part of it—its ideas, stories, and practices—can be copied, remixed, and passed on. Knowledge thrives when it moves, evolves, and inspires. If this book sparks something in you, let it spread. The only request is to honor those who brought this wisdom forward—give credit where credit is due, acknowledge the sources, and keep the spirit of sharing alive.

Let's choose evolution over stagnation. Keep the conversation going.

CONTENTS

Acknowledgements

No act of humanity happens in isolation, and neither does the creation of a book. This guide exists because of the love, wisdom, and support of so many people who have shaped my life and work.

To my family—thank you for being my roots and my resilience. A special thanks to my Grandma Jo, my Dad Sam, and my cousins Brianna, Eric, Tyler, Jennifer, Shannon, and Sylvia. To my great-aunt Shirley, whose kindness echoes through generations, and my nephew Zak, who reminds me that the future is bright—I am grateful for you all.

To Tim, my partner of almost 17 years (and counting), who goes above and beyond to try and understand me, loving me in both subversive and overt ways. Your patience, care, and quiet acts of devotion sustain me more than words can express.

To Zeshan Asghar—thank you for your skillful guidance in refining and formatting this book. You not only helped shape these musings into something more accessible but also walked me through my first self-publishing journey with patience and encouragement.

To Jane Goodall, Frans de Waal, and the many brilliant primatologists who have spent their lives observing and learning from our fellow primates. Your work has illuminated the deep, ancient roots of empathy, cooperation, and care—proving that kindness is not just human, but woven into the very fabric of our evolutionary story. Thank you for reminding us that to understand ourselves, we must first understand the creatures who share our world.

To the ancestor Martha Graham, who reminds us that "no artist is ever satisfied." May the restless, relentless creative spirit continue to push us toward deeper expression, knowing that the work is never done—only ever evolving.

And to every reader who picks up this guide—you are part of this story, too. May these words inspire you to embrace kindness as both an art and an act of quiet rebellion.

Ever yours, a conspirator in humanity,

Ken

Prelude to the Subversive

Now reread that. Let it sit with you for a moment.

I am a humble first-time author, a proud American of Irish-German mixed heritage, raised in rural Pennsylvania. A pale-skinned, queer, middle-aged man who deeply respects Martin Luther King Jr.'s *I Have a Dream* legacy. And yet, here I am, opening this book with the opposite—a nightmare. One so vivid, absurd, and unsettling that it jolted me awake, heart pounding, sweat-soaked, knowing my psyche had crossed a line.

In this night terror, I stood in the Rose Garden on a perfect spring day, the air thick with the scent of fresh blossoms. It should have been a scene of renewal, of possibility. But instead—chaos. A massive, belligerent, obese orangutan—fur matted, face twisted in a grotesque snarl—was flinging shit at everyone in sight. He was relentless. Screeching, thrashing, desecrating every inch of what should have been sacred ground. And the worst part? No one was stopping him. Some watched in stunned silence. Others, incredibly, cheered.

I woke up rattled, my body still trapped in the grip of the nightmare. Disoriented, I stumbled into the bathroom, flipped on the light, and did what humans have done for generations in moments of existential crisis—I splashed cold water on my face. Again and again. Anything to shake off the lingering dread. Finally, I looked into the mirror, locking eyes with my own reflection, and whispered, *It was just a dream. A really bad dream.*

But was it? Because the nightmare didn't end when I opened my eyes.

As I stood there, still dripping, something stirred in the back of my mind—a memory from childhood. The first time I watched the original *King Kong*. Even as an ape-loving kid, I was terrified of the claymation monstrosity. His jerky, unnatural movements, his eerie, exaggerated face—it wasn't the awe-inspiring majesty of the great apes I had come to admire. It was something else. Something unsettling. Something *wrong*. And yet, by the end of the movie, I felt something I didn't expect: pity.

Because Kong didn't deserve his fate. He was a misunderstood creature, hunted down for simply existing. His demise was a manufactured tragedy, orchestrated by those who saw him as a monster rather than a being worthy of compassion.

But this current tragedy? It's real. And it isn't the story of one misplaced giant—it's the story of a world being led off a cliff by an entire system built to prioritize power, profit, and spectacle over people.

In real life, an equally bloated, belligerent, disrespectful, orange-tinged primate had taken up residence in the White House. And unlike King Kong—who, let's be honest, was just trying to survive in a world that feared him—this apex manipulator isn't some hapless victim. This one relishes the destruction. If, by sheer accident, he happened to do something for the greater good, it would be as coincidental as King Kong redesigning the Empire State Building while climbing it in self-defense.

We, as a species, are hitting a wall. Our collective psyche is breaking under the weight of our own hubris, our disconnection, our inability to see beyond the myths we've been sold. We are primates with technology too advanced for our emotional intelligence, still clinging to hierarchies, still mistaking dominance for strength, still failing to evolve where it matters most.

So what do we do? How do we break free from this nightmare?

We start by dreaming. Not passively. Not with wistful longing. But with subversive, deliberate, creative acts of resistance. With the kind of dreaming that stirs revolutions—not just in the streets, but in our hearts, our minds, our relationships, our daily interactions. The kind of dreaming that turns the tools of oppression into instruments of liberation.

This book is my offering. My small act of defiance against despair. A collection of subversive strategies—some ancient, some radical, all within reach—that, applied with intention, might just help us untangle ourselves from this mess.

Little by little, person by person, action by action, we can wake up. We can reclaim our humanity. We can rewrite the story.

But first, we must have the courage to dream.

And then, the willingness to act.

This is not a drill. This is not a dream. This is our wake-up call.

Let's answer it.

Introduction:

Subversive Acts of Humanity

Welcome to *Subversive Acts of Humanity: A Survival Guide for Choosing Evolution Over Self-Destruction.* This is more than a guide for survival—it's a call to reclaim our humanity and thrive during one of the most turbulent periods in history. The crises we face— environmental destruction, rising inequality, fractured societies, and a crisis of meaning—are daunting. But we are not powerless.

Right now, humanity is at a crossroads. We are sliding headfirst into a self-inflicted dark age. Yet, at this very moment, we are also on the cusp of something extraordinary: the potential to evolve. The path we choose will shape the future of our species and the planet itself.

A WORD ON POWER-HUNGRY BABOONS (AND WHY THEY DESERVE BETTER THAN THIS COMPARISON)

This book is not for those who thrive on oppression, control, and hoarding resources while the rest of us struggle. It is not for the corporate overlords, the political strongmen, or the tech billionaires playing God with their unearned influence.

Some might call these people **power-hungry baboons**, but frankly, that's an insult to baboons. At least real baboons know how to lead within their own social structures. Their hierarchies—though rigid—serve a function in their troop. Alpha baboons **protect** their community, share resources (to an extent), and engage in elaborate social grooming that reinforces connection.

When an alpha loses their strength or abuses their role, they get overthrown, often dramatically, but fairly. Compare that to human leaders who cling to power at all costs, build systems that ensure their dominance, and leave the weak to suffer.

So, no, this book isn't for **them**. Nor is it for those whose psychological wounds run so deep that they cannot comprehend its message. They are not our enemies, but they are the reason this book exists.

And with that, I offer a **subversive THANK YOU** to those who have inspired this book—not with their wisdom, but with their failures. Their greed, cruelty, and short-sightedness have made it clearer than ever that we need a different way forward.

THIS BOOK IS FOR YOU

This book is for those of us who feel the weight of what's happening but don't know where to begin. It's for the rebels, the dreamers, and the truth-tellers who refuse to accept the status quo. It's a guide to help us evolve into something greater: perhaps *Homo cordis*, defined by compassion, empathy, and love. Or *Homo animus,* deeply attuned to the Earth, harmonizing intellect with instinct. Perhaps the future holds elements of both.

The truth is, **evolution doesn't wait**. It requires action. And this book is a call to subversion: **small, radical acts that defy a broken system and create ripples of change.**

WHY THIS MATTERS

The dark age we're entering isn't a distant threat—it's already here. Species are disappearing. Forests are vanishing. Inequality is rising. Political and cultural divides have deepened to the point of fracture. Many people feel spiritually disconnected, unsure of where to turn. It's tempting to give in to apathy or despair, to believe that chaos is inevitable. But I refuse to accept that.

Change doesn't begin with grand gestures—it starts with us. The quiet revolutions in how we **live, love, and connect** have the power to reshape everything. Small acts of kindness. Radical self-love. Fierce truth-telling. These are antidotes to the despair that threatens to consume us.

THE NEUROSCIENCE OF SUBVERSION: WHY SMALL ACTS MATTER IN DARK TIMES

When people feel **powerless**, their nervous system enters **fight, flight, freeze, or fawn** mode. And let's be honest—our society is designed to keep people frozen in **despair** or fawning in **compliance**. Overworked, underpaid, overstimulated, and exhausted—we are easier to control when we believe we can't change anything.

Subversive acts are a **biological rebellion**. They interrupt these fear-based responses and activate **neuroplasticity**—our brain's ability to rewire itself. **Every** small act of defiance, joy, and connection strengthens neural pathways for resilience, courage, and critical thinking.

Neuroscience tells us that the **ventral vagal system** (responsible for social connection and safety) is crucial for both **individual well-being and collective resistance.** When we engage in **acts of kindness, creative defiance, and community-building,** we activate this system. The result? We feel **empowered rather than helpless, connected rather than isolated.**

In short: **subversive acts rewire your brain for hope, agency, and action.** They are the first steps toward real change.

A PLANET OF APES, OURSELVES

For better or worse, we are still just apes. Technologically advanced, emotionally volatile, and socially confused apes.

We've built cities, AI, and global networks, but our core instincts remain the same as those of our primate relatives. Chimps show us the dangers of unchecked dominance, war, and greed. Bonobos, on the other hand, live in societies based on cooperation, pleasure, and peace. **We have a choice.**

Do we continue down the path of **Homo destructus,** consuming everything until there's nothing left? Or do we lean into our capacity for compassion, interdependence, and balance?

What if *Homo sapiens*—the so-called "wise human"—has reached its limits? We've mastered technology, reshaped landscapes, and stretched our dominion across the Earth, yet we remain trapped in cycles of fear, greed, and destruction. Evolution is inevitable—but where do we go from here?

This is just a concept, an idea, a hypothesis. But what if the next step isn't about intelligence alone, but about expanding our capacity for connection, intuition, and balance?

Do we evolve into Homo cordis—the "humans of the heart," prioritizing compassion and interdependence? Do we become Homo animus—the "humans of the soul," deeply attuned to creativity, inner wisdom, and the rhythms of the universe? Or is the next phase something beyond what we can yet conceive?

This isn't a prophecy, just a possibility. But if we're the ones shaping evolution, what kind of humans do we want to be?

SURVIVAL IS EVOLUTION

If we survive, we will evolve. Evolution isn't about clinging to what is—it's about becoming something new. Imagine Homo cordis et animus, a species that balances **love, intellect, and ecological harmony.** Imagine cities that resemble forests, technologies that heal rather than harm, and societies rooted in balance and cooperation.

This is more than a dream. **It's the logical outcome of choosing to evolve.** And evolution begins with the individual.

CHANGING THE WORLD ONE SUBVERSIVE ACT AT A TIME

The change we need isn't about waiting for someone else to act—it's about embracing our own power. **Subversive acts—kindness, self-love, advocacy—are small, but they ripple outward. They create movements. They dismantle systems that no longer serve us.**

This book will guide you through **15 subversive acts** designed to help you thrive and transform. From embracing your inner wildness to redefining how you connect with others, these practices will challenge you to think, act, and live differently.

A NEW NARRATIVE

This isn't just a survival guide. **It's an invitation to reimagine what it means to be human.**

Drawing on my experiences as a **yoga therapist, social worker, psychedelic integration specialist, and budding primatologist,** I'll help you reclaim your **primal instincts** in ways that heal both yourself and the world.

Our closest relatives—chimps, gorillas, bonobos, and orangutans—teach us about **cooperation, care, and resilience.** Their behaviors remind us that the answers to our current crises might lie **not in outsmarting nature but in learning from it.**

We must **unlearn the habits of disconnection and fear** that have shaped us. **Radical acts of kindness, fierce self-love, and subversive activism** are our tools to combat the cynicism that permeates society. Together, they can create the **ripple effect that transforms the world.**

EMBRACING THE SHADOWS

Subversion isn't always comfortable. **Confronting the darkness—both within and around us—requires courage.** Carl Jung's concept of **shadow work** reminds us that transformation only comes from **facing what we fear most.**

The world is watching. The future is unwritten. And we are the authors of what comes next.

And if the power-hungry baboons of our world don't like it?

To that, I offer a heartfelt, deeply evolved, **bonobo-inspired kiss of defiance.**

Now, let's get to work.

WHAT KIND OF APE ARE YOU?

Let's be real—if you're reading this, you're an ape. Yes, an ape. Whether you like the *Planet of the Apes* franchise or not, it's a fact: Homo sapiens is a species of great ape.

SPOILER ALERT: Throughout this book, we'll be doing some mirror work—because survival isn't just about endurance, it's about seeing ourselves clearly. And that?

That's revolutionary. Self-recognition is a subversive act. Only a few species dare to look in the mirror and truly see themselves—great apes, dolphins, elephants, magpies... and, if we're willing, us. But here's the catch: once we see, we can't unsee.

So, before we begin, let's ask ourselves: Are we ready to face the reflection? Because this isn't just a guide book. It's a reckoning.

Now comes the fun part—what kind of ape are you? This isn't about labels or judgment but an invitation to reflect on who you are at your core and how you move through the world. It's also a reminder that we humans, while boasting our oversized brains, share this planet with four other incredible ape species. And, let's face it, they have some lessons to teach us.

Take a moment to connect with your inner primate. No quizzes, no scoring—just a chance to tune into your instincts, your relationships, and your energy. Call it a hunch or an intuitive leap. Let's explore the great apes and see which one resonates with you. Along the way, I'll share some stories from my own journey to meet these magnificent beings in their natural habitats—a privilege that has deeply shaped my understanding of our interconnectedness.

GORILLA

- **Group Name:** Stable Troops, Harem-Based Structure

- **Traits:** Calm, grounded, and fiercely family-oriented.

- **Habitat:** Gorillas live in tight-knit troops led by a dominant silverback. These groups are built on trust, cooperation, and care, often consisting of one male, several females, and their offspring.

- **Strengths:** Gentle giants with a strong sense of loyalty and protection. Gorillas value peace and avoid conflict unless their loved ones are threatened.

- **Challenges:** Sensitive to environmental changes and slow to adapt. They thrive in stability but can struggle when their routines are disrupted.

- **Reflection:** If you see yourself in gorillas, you might prioritize harmony and family bonds. But perhaps you could also challenge yourself to embrace change and step out of your comfort zone.

Inspiring Moment: Visiting the mountain gorillas of Uganda in the Bwindi Impenetrable Forest was like stepping into another world. These majestic creatures, with their soulful eyes and quiet strength, embody a peace that feels ancient. I was particularly moved by the public health initiative in the area—farmers relocating to allow the rainforest to expand for the gorillas' growing population. During COVID-19, when humans stayed away, there was a gorilla baby boom.

Proof that when we give nature the space to heal, it doesn't just survive—it thrives. A paradox we must hold: while we humans struggled and suffered when COVID arrived at our doorsteps, the natural world exhaled. The gorillas flourished, the skies cleared, the forests deepened. What might we learn from this? What happens when we step back, listen, and let both the wild world and our own untamed selves breathe?

CHIMPANZEE

- **Group Name:** Fission-Fusion, Male-Dominated Hierarchy

- **Traits:** Social, playful, and intensely curious.

- **Habitat:** Chimpanzees thrive in larger, complex communities with intricate social hierarchies. They are constantly forging alliances, learning, and teaching.

- **Strengths:** Chimps are highly innovative, known for their ability to use tools and solve problems. They work together to hunt, share resources, and navigate group dynamics.

- **Challenges:** Their passion can sometimes spill over into aggression. They're capable of both great collaboration and intense conflict, even within their own group.

- **Reflection:** If you resonate with chimps, you may be a natural problem-solver who thrives in social settings. Your challenge may be learning to temper competitiveness and channel your passion into collaboration.

Inspiring Moment: In Uganda, I trekked through the forests of Kibale National Park to see chimps in action.

Watching them crack nuts with rocks and engage in elaborate grooming rituals was a reminder of their brilliance and complexity. They are so much like us— the good, the bad, and everything in between. Chimps are a mirror reflecting our own potential for connection and conflict, depending on how we choose to live.

BONOBO

- **Group Name:** Fission-Fusion, Matriarchal Society

- **Traits:** Peaceful, empathetic, and joyfully playful.

- **Habitat:** Bonobos live in female-led groups that prioritize harmony over hierarchy. Their lives are built on connection, affection, and cooperation.

- **Strengths:** Known as the "hippie apes," bonobos resolve tension through touch, play, and physical closeness. They are masters of peace-building and inclusion.

- **Challenges:** While their focus on harmony is beautiful, it can leave them vulnerable in competitive or aggressive situations.

- **Reflection:** If bonobos speak to your soul, you might value connection, peace, and inclusivity. Your growth edge may involve learning to balance harmony with the ability to set boundaries and assert your needs.

Inspiring Hope: While I haven't yet visited bonobos in their natural habitats, I dream of the day. Bonobos are only found in the Democratic Republic of Congo, where efforts to protect them continue despite immense challenges. For a long time, we didn't even realize bonobos and chimpanzees were separate species—just lumped them together as one. But when we finally paid attention, we saw the difference: one built a society on dominance and conflict, the other on pleasure and peace. What else might we be missing by not looking closer?

Bonobos remind us that gentleness and cooperation aren't weaknesses—they're evolutionary superpowers. So, what if we looked at ourselves with the same fresh eyes? What if we questioned the stories we've been told about survival, strength, and success? What might we discover about who we really are—and who we could become?

ORANGUTAN

- **Group Name:** Solitary or Loose Networks (mothers and offspring form tight bonds)

- **Traits:** Independent, introspective, and deliberate.

- **Habitat:** Orangutans are the great philosophers of the ape world, living solitary lives in the lush forests of Southeast Asia. They spend most of their time in trees, crafting elaborate nests and observing the world.

- **Strengths:** Deep thinkers and master strategists, orangutans use tools and creativity to solve problems with remarkable precision.

- **Challenges:** Their independence can sometimes lead to isolation. While they value solitude, they also thrive on the occasional connection.

- **Reflection:** If you feel a kinship with orangutans, you may be someone who treasures quiet reflection and self-reliance. Your challenge may be finding ways to stay connected to others without losing your sense of individuality.

Inspiring Moment: Seeing orangutans in the forests of Borneo was unforgettable. These wise and graceful beings, swinging effortlessly through the canopy, radiate an ancient, contemplative energy. They are incredibly devoted to their young, teaching them how to survive in a world that continues to shrink due to human encroachment. Orangutans remind us of the power of deliberate action and the beauty of taking time to simply be.

A CALL TO ACTION

Homo sapiens has long considered itself the "crown jewel" of evolution, but perhaps we've been missing the point. We've spent so much time trying to dominate the natural world that we've forgotten how to learn from it. This is your invitation to tap into your inner ape and rethink what it means to be human.

Whether you see yourself as a gorilla, chimp, bonobo, or orangutan—or a blend of all four—remember that each species holds wisdom for us. Gorillas teach us loyalty, chimps inspire ingenuity, bonobos show us the power of peace, and orangutans remind us to honor quiet strength.

If this feels like a lighthearted exercise, let it be the first test of your ability to step into a new paradigm. The goal here isn't to categorize or rank yourself (that would be a very Homo sapiens thing to do). Instead, use this as a playful reflection to guide your journey through this book—and perhaps your journey beyond it.

We are entering a critical time for our species, and our survival depends on whether we can evolve into something more compassionate, connected, and conscious. Call it Homo cordis et animus. Call it the next chapter. Whatever you call it, the world needs you to bring your inner primate wisdom to life.

So, fellow ape, let's swing boldly into the future together. Whether you choose to groom, climb, nap, or build, you are part of this wild and beautiful story. Welcome to the (r)evolution.

SUBVERSIVE ACT: MIRROR, MIRROR, WHO'S THAT PRIMATE?

Before we go any further, let's test what we have covered so far with some mirror work. Put this book down. No, really—put it down. Stand up or sit in front of a mirror. Look yourself in the eyes. Just breathe and observe.

Something happens when we see ourselves reflected back. We recognize, judge, analyze, and sometimes even avoid our own gaze. Mirrors are portals to self-awareness, but also to illusion. The version of you in the mirror is both real and not real—a shifting perception of self that changes with time, mood, and perspective.

Now, let's strip away the layers of civilization for a moment. Look at yourself and say out loud: "I am an ape."

Say it again. Louder. Feel the words. "I AM AN APE."

Now, don't just say it—be it. Let yourself move, grunt, scratch, tilt your head, bare your teeth, puff out your chest, swing your arms. Feel your body. Feel your instincts. Try this for at least three minutes.

What happens when you stop trying to be human and let yourself be a primate? Do you feel ridiculous? Liberated? Embodied?

When you're ready, come back to the book. But don't come back the same. Bring your inner ape with you.

WE'VE HAD OUR WARM UP LAP - NOW YOU'RE PRIMED, I AM PUMPED! ONWARD WE GO!

This book is an invitation to embrace your primal wisdom and use it to create change. By challenging societal norms and practicing radical compassion, we can build a future defined by love, justice, and connection.

You are the hero of this story. Your subversive acts matter. Together, we can evolve into a species that thrives—not in spite of our challenges, but because of them.

Let's rewrite this story, one subversive act at a time.

Chapter 1:

Ape-solutely Kind

"

> "My wish for you is that you continue. Continue to be who and how you are, to astonish a mean world with your acts of kindness. Continue to allow humor to lighten the burden of your tender heart."
>
> **- Maya Angelou**

SUBVERSIVE ACT #1

Spread kindness through small, genuine acts of care and connection, while honoring your limits and practicing kindness toward yourself.

INTRODUCTION: WHY BONOBOS INSPIRE US

 Let's start our journey with a foundational principle: kindness. Among our closest living relatives, bonobos stand out as a species defined by empathy, cooperation, and connection. Unlike chimpanzees, bonobos live in peaceful, matriarchal societies where affection and collaboration, rather than aggression, are the norm.

Discovered relatively late in the 20th century, bonobos were initially mistaken for chimpanzees until pioneering research by scientists like Frans de Waal revealed their unique behaviors (de Waal, 1997). Bonobos teach us an essential truth: kindness is not a weakness but a survival strategy.

In bonobo groups, individuals comfort one another through hugs, kisses, and grooming. They share food willingly, even with strangers, fostering trust and cooperation (Hare, 2020). If these "hippie apes" can thrive through compassion, so can we. As Aesop reminds us, "No act of kindness, no matter how small, is ever wasted."

For humans, kindness often feels radical in a world that glorifies individualism and competition. Yet, as I experienced firsthand during my first trip to go food shopping during the 2020 "sheltering in place" era, kindness can also be exhausting.

By the time I navigated the shared foraging space, weaving through masked faces filled with quiet distress, I felt the weight of collective anxiety pressing in. So few strangers were willing to make eye contact—everyone was fending for themselves, lost in their own silent battles. Small gestures of warmth—holding a door, offering a nod of reassurance—felt necessary but left me completely drained.

Then, as I reached my car, fumbling with my bags, a stranger silently steadied my cart and met my eyes with a look that said, *"We're all in this together."* A fleeting moment, but in a time of isolation, that small act of solidarity felt like a lifeline.

Moments like that taught me that kindness must also be sustainable. Like bonobos, who balance generosity with rest and connection, we must remember that caring for ourselves is part of the equation. This chapter is about embracing kindness as a subversive act-one that strengthens our shared humanity while acknowledging our individual limits.

PRIMATE CONNECTION: THE POWER OF KINDNESS IN BONOBO SOCIETIES

 Bonobos are a testament to the evolutionary value of kindness. They:

✓ Resolve conflicts with affection: Instead of resorting to aggression, bonobos use physical closeness, such as grooming and touch, to diffuse tensions (White, 1996).

✓ Create harmony through matriarchal leadership: Female bonobos form alliances that promote social stability and cooperation (Hare, 2020).

✓ Demonstrate generosity: Bonobos share food and resources with their group members and even with those outside their immediate circle (Tan & Hare, 2013).

These behaviors aren't just "nice"; they're survival strategies. By prioritizing connection and care, bonobos thrive in a way that offers profound lessons for humanity. Imagine what we could achieve by adopting similar principles in our daily lives.

A HUMAN STORY: THE RIPPLE EFFECT OF SMALL ACTS

 During one particularly difficult week, I stopped at a local café for a moment of calm. The barista looked visibly overwhelmed, juggling orders and spills behind the counter. When she apologized for the wait, I smiled and said, "You're doing great. Take your time."

She paused, visibly startled, and smiled back. "Thank you," she said softly, her shoulders visibly relaxing.

When she handed me my coffee, she added, "This one's on me."

That small exchange reminded me that kindness doesn't have to be grandiose. It lives in simple gestures, like a patient smile or a word of encouragement. Kindness isn't just a one-way street-it ripples outward, often returning to us in unexpected ways.

DARK THOUGHT EXPERIMENT

 Imagine a world where kindness is extinct. People rush past one another, heads down, disconnected and indifferent. Small acts of care-holding a door, offering a smile, or lending a helping hand-are forgotten. Relationships grow cold, communities dissolve, and the warmth of human connection fades entirely.

Now imagine the opposite: a world where kindness thrives. Strangers greet each other warmly, friends offer help without hesitation, and every small act of care strengthens the fabric of society. Which world do you want to live in? What can you do today to bring more kindness into your corner of the world?

WHEN YOU'RE TOO TIRED TO BE KIND

There will be days when offering kindness to others feels impossible. On those days, remember: kindness begins within. Dr. Martha Beck's practice of KIST (Kind

Internal Self-Talk) offers a powerful way to care for yourself:

- When negative self-talk creeps in, pause.
- Speak to yourself as you would a dear friend, offering phrases like, "You're doing your best," or, "It's okay to rest today."
- Reflect on what you truly need in that moment and give yourself permission to honor it.

By practicing kindness toward ourselves, we refill our emotional reserves. Together, these acts create what I call a kinder garden- a space where empathy, connection, and self-care can flourish side by side.

INTERACTIVE EXERCISES

1. The Compliment Challenge

Each day this week, offer at least one genuine compliment to someone around you. Be specific and observe how it's received.

2. Kindness Journal

At the end of each day, write down one act of kindness you gave and one you received. Reflect on how these moments shaped your day and your mood.

3. Circle Back to Yourself

On days when kindness feels overwhelming, practice KIST. Write down three supportive, kind statements for yourself, such as, "I am allowed to rest," or, "I am enough as I am." Reflect on how this changes your mood.

4. Kindness Ripple Tracker

Track the ripple effects of your kindness. Did someone pass it on? How far did your small act travel? If you can't actually track it, how can you imagine the ripple effects of how you paid it forward? Sometimes the impact of a single gesture extends beyond what we can see—but that doesn't mean it isn't shaping the world in ways we'll never fully know.

EVIDENCE-BASED PRACTICES

Loving-Kindness Meditation

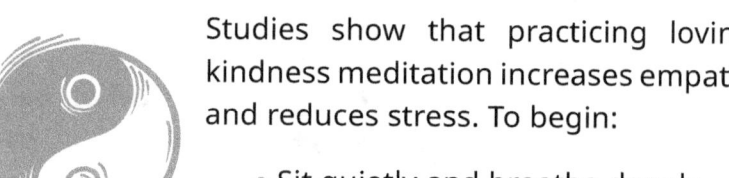 Studies show that practicing loving-kindness meditation increases empathy and reduces stress. To begin:

- Sit quietly and breathe deeply.
- Start with yourself, silently repeating, "May I be happy. May I be healthy. May I be at peace."
- Extend these wishes to others-friends, family, even strangers: "May you be happy. May you be healthy. May you be at peace."

Mindful Acts of Kindness

Mindful kindness-offering care with full presence-amplifies its impact on both the giver and receiver.

REFLECTION QUESTIONS

1. How does practicing kindness, whether toward yourself or others, impact your emotional well-being?

2. What fears or insecurities hold you back from showing kindness more openly?

3. What is one small act of kindness you can try this week to create a ripple effect in your community?

CONCLUSION

Kindness is more than a virtue-it's a survival strategy. Bonobos remind us that care and connection form the foundation of thriving communities. For humans, kindness connects us to others, builds trust, and leaves a lasting impression.

When kindness toward others feels too heavy, circle back to your own heart. Together, we can create a kinder garden-one small act, one gentle word, one moment of compassion at a time.

We may not know exactly what thoughts run through the minds of our great ape relatives, but we do know they are capable of remarkable kindness. Across species, across circumstances, we have observed apes offering comfort, forming deep bonds, and even going out of their way to help those in need.

Take, for example, Binti Jua, the Western Lowland Gorilla at the Brookfield Zoo. In 1996, when a three-year-old human child fell into her enclosure, she didn't react with aggression or indifference. Instead, she gently picked him up, cradled him, and carried him to safety, protecting him until zoo staff could reach him. Her instinct wasn't to harm—it was to help.

Acts like these remind us that compassion is not just a human invention; it is a deeply rooted part of our primate nature. We are not alone in our capacity to care, to soothe, to offer kindness. And if our great ape cousins can show such tenderness, then surely, we too can choose to be a little gentler with ourselves.

So go back to the mirror. Look yourself in the eyes. And this time, fill your reflection with words of kindness. Ape-solutely kinder we can be.

Chapter 2:

Rewilding Your Inner Chimp

"

"*In every walk with nature, one receives far more than he seeks.*"

- John Muir

SUBVERSIVE ACT #2

Disconnect from the human-made world to rediscover your primal instincts and natural rhythm.

INTRODUCTION: RECONNECTING WITH THE WILD WITHIN

 Modern life has domesticated us. We wake to alarms, live by schedules, and often feel disconnected from the natural rhythms that sustained our ancestors for millennia. In our quest for convenience, we've built a "human zoo," caging ourselves in routines, technology, and artificial environments. But deep within us, there's still a wildness—a primal instinct waiting to be unleashed.

Our closest primate relatives, such as bonobos and chimpanzees, thrive in the wild, responding to natural rhythms, forging complex social bonds, and engaging in playful exploration. Yet, when placed in captivity, their behavior shifts dramatically. Apes in enclosures, deprived of the stimulation of the natural world, often develop stress-related behaviors like pacing, rocking, or social withdrawal. Their instincts don't vanish—they lie dormant, waiting for the right conditions to reawaken.

Humans, too, suffer from a similar captivity. While our enclosures may look like skyscrapers, fluorescent-lit offices, and digital screens, the effects are no less profound. Rewilding isn't about abandoning modern life but about rediscovering the rhythms and instincts that make us feel alive. As Julia Plevin in *The Healing*

Magic of Forest Bathing shared: "Forest bathing is a process of rewilding, simultaneously the most natural and the hardest thing. It's a stomping out of all our learned behaviors so we can reacquaint with our true selves and, with that, the web that comprises every living thing."

PRIMATE CONNECTION: BONOBOS AND CHIMPS IN THE WILD VS. CAPTIVITY

 Apes provide a striking example of how environment shapes behavior:

✓ **In the wild:** Bonobos and chimpanzees forage for food, climb trees, and use tools to solve problems, stimulating their brains and bodies. They build rich social lives, maintaining bonds through grooming, play, and cooperation.

✓ **In captivity:** Deprived of these natural stimuli, apes may develop stereotypic behaviors like pacing, repetitive rocking, or social withdrawal— signs of mental distress caused by boredom and lack of stimulation (Mallapur, 2005). Social groupings are often disrupted, leading to isolation or aggression (De Waal, 1982).

However, here's the hopeful part: when apes are reintroduced to natural habitats, they often relearn their instincts. They climb, forage, and interact as they once did, proving that their wild essence remains intact. For humans, the lesson is clear: even in the most structured, technological lives, our primal instincts are waiting to be reawakened.

A HUMAN STORY: FROM MULCH TO MAGIC

Before the pandemic, I started dabbling with plants, tending to a modest yard with some mulch and succulents. COVID-19 turned the world upside down for most, and it also helped many of us turn inward. As part of my sanity maintenance plan, I leaned into a quieter connection with nature. Over the past five years, my small experiment has blossomed into a thriving ecosystem.

Today, what was once a barren patch of earth is now alive with hummingbirds and butterflies, an orchid thriving where I never thought it could, and fruit trees overflowing with peaches, persimmons, and pomegranates. It didn't take much money, just time, energy, and the willingness to observe and care for the life around me.

The most profound part? Sharing the abundance. When the harvest exceeds what my family can eat, we pass the fruit to neighbors who, in turn, help tend the wilder parts of the yard when we're away. This small act of giving reminds me of the lessons from Chapter 1: kindness and connection, even with the natural world, create ripples that go far beyond ourselves.

DARK THOUGHT EXPERIMENT

 Imagine a world where humans are completely "captive." Cities stretch endlessly, green spaces vanish, and every activity takes place indoors. There's no place to wander, no trees to climb, and no birds to hear. Over time, people lose their creativity, vitality, and sense of freedom. What happens to the human spirit in such a world?

Now imagine the opposite: a world where humans are free to roam in nature, create with their hands, and connect with their surroundings. What kind of person would you become in that world? How can you bring that freedom into your life today?

INTERACTIVE EXERCISES

1.   Watch Wild Behavior

 Choose a documentary about bonobos, chimpanzees, or another species that fascinates you. Pay attention to how they interact with their environment and each other. Write down three behaviors that inspire you and think of ways to replicate them in your life (e.g., playful movement, problem-solving, or cooperation).

2. Break Free from a Routine

Identify one part of your daily routine that feels confining or monotonous. Replace it with a "rewilding" activity, like a walk in the park, an impromptu climb, or unstructured play. Reflect on how this change impacts your mood and energy.

3. Create a Rewilding Space

Design a small part of your home or yard to mimic the natural world. Add plants, natural textures, and elements that stimulate your senses, such as rocks, water, or sand. Use this space for quiet reflection or playful exploration.

4. Forest Bathing

Inspired by the Japanese practice of shinrin-yoku, take a slow, mindful walk in a forest or park. Focus on your senses—notice the colors, sounds, and smells around you. Let nature ground and rejuvenate you.

EVIDENCE-BASED PRACTICES

1. Nature Therapy

Research shows that spending time in nature reduces stress, lowers blood pressure, and improves mood. Plan a weekly "nature date" with yourself. Spend one to two hours in a natural setting, free from distractions, and notice how it affects your mind and body.

2. Movement for Rewilding

Studies confirm that natural movement—walking, climbing, or even crawling—activates muscles and neural pathways that modern life often neglects. Incorporate primal movements into your day. Stretch on the floor, squat while cooking, or climb a tree.

3. Earthing or Grounding

Physical contact with the earth has been shown to reduce inflammation, improve sleep, and boost well-being. Walk barefoot on clean grass, sand, or soil for at least 15 minutes daily, but take precautions to avoid infections, sharp objects, or allergens. Wash your feet afterward, especially if you have cuts or a weakened immune system. Those with circulation issues should check for injuries post-grounding. If outdoor grounding isn't an option, grounding mats can provide a similar effect indoors.

REFLECTION QUESTIONS

1. How often do you engage with nature in meaningful ways? What barriers prevent you from doing so more often?

2. What primal activities—play, movement, or exploration—bring you the most joy? How can you incorporate them into your routine?

3. How would rewilding your life change your physical, emotional, and social well-being?

4. After watching a documentary on apes or other animals, what new perspectives did you gain about the natural world and your connection to it?

CONCLUSION

 When apes are removed from captivity and reintroduced to the wild, they often relearn natural behaviors—climbing, foraging, and social bonding—proving that wild instincts never truly disappear. The same is true for us.

By stepping out of our mental and physical cages, we can rediscover the joy, creativity, and vitality that come from living as nature intended. Rewilding isn't just about escaping our enclosures; it's about remembering who we are at our core. Like our revolutionary kin, we are meant to move, play, explore, and connect. So, let's take inspiration from the wild, reintroduce ourselves to our natural rhythms, and create a world where freedom and vitality thrive.

Chapter 3:

Radical Rest in the Canopy

"

> "Rest is not idleness, and to lie sometimes on the grass under trees on a summer's day, listening to the murmur of water, or watching the clouds float across the sky, is by no means a waste of time."
>
> **- John Lubbock**

SUBVERSIVE ACT

Reclaim rest as a revolutionary act in a world that glorifies busyness.

INTRODUCTION: THE FORGOTTEN POWER OF REST

 Let's face it: in our culture, busyness is often worn as a badge of honor. The phrase "I'm so busy" is thrown around like a mark of importance. But this constant hustle is wearing us down, making us irritable, less creative, and—ironically—less productive. Meanwhile, in the animal kingdom, rest is sacred.

Take mountain gorillas, for example. They aren't rushing around worrying about deadlines or whether they're productive enough. Between foraging sessions, they stretch out in sun-dappled meadows or recline under the shade of trees with their troop. Not because they're lazy, but because they know that energy conservation and social connection are just as vital as action.

And what about orangutans? These master architects build elaborate tree nests every evening, prioritizing comfort and safety for their nightly rest. No scrolling through their phones before bed. No stressing about tomorrow's banana quotas. They invest in quality rest because it sustains them.

So why do we humans struggle with rest? We've been taught to believe it as indulgent, even irresponsible. (Instead of "see" consider using "believe") But rest is revolutionary—it defies the pressure to always be "on" and reminds us that we're human, not machines. As your friendly guide to all things primal, I'm here to tell you: it's time to reclaim rest as an essential, subversive act.

PRIMATE CONNECTION: RESTING PATTERNS ACROSS SPECIES

Rest is hardwired into our primate relatives:

- ✓ **Mountain Gorillas:** After a morning of foraging, gorillas lounge together as a family. It's not just about conserving energy—it's about reinforcing social bonds. A napping gorilla is often leaning against another for warmth and comfort.

- ✓ **Orangutans:** These arboreal geniuses take bedtime seriously. Their tree nests are feats of engineering, woven with strong branches and cushioned with leaves. If orangutans can treat their rest like an art form, maybe we can put a little more effort into our sleep routines too.

- ✓ **Chimpanzees:** Chimps don't just rest—they make it social. They nap close to their allies, turning rest into a trust-building activity.

- ✓ **Bonobos:** True to their affectionate nature, bonobos mix rest with connection, often cuddling or grooming while lounging. Rest isn't just about recovery; it's about reinforcing bonds.

Even domesticated animals remind us of rest's importance. Dogs snooze for 10–14 hours a day, and cats? They're practically professional nappers, clocking in 16 hours daily. These creatures don't feel guilty about rest, so why should we?

A HUMAN STORY: LEARNING TO NAP, LEARNING TO THRIVE

I never thought I'd need to teach myself how to nap, but here I am, an adult who finally figured it out. For years, I struggled with insomnia—falling asleep was hard, and staying asleep was even harder. But as I grew older, I realized how transformative rest could be, even in small doses.

One day, out of sheer exhaustion, I decided to try a 10-minute nap. I set a timer, lay down, and let myself doze. When I woke up, it was as though someone had hit the reset button in my brain. I felt clear-headed, calm, and ready to face the day. That one small experiment turned into a habit. Now, I look forward to my "micro-naps," those little bursts of rest that recharge me like nothing else.

I also leaned into **yoga nidra**, a guided meditation practice often called "yogic sleep." It became my go-to tool for those restless nights when my inner "worrier" wouldn't let me drift off. Instead of fighting my sleeplessness, I'd turn on a yoga nidra session and let my body relax, even if my mind couldn't fully shut down. A quick search on any of the song or podcast apps or YouTube will help you find a treasure chest of FREE recordings of this evidence-based practice. The fun can be in finding the right voice, length and tempo of a yoga nidra that might work best for you!

And let's talk about mornings. I used to rely on the snooze button like it was my best friend, but it turns out, snoozing does more harm than good. Those extra fragmented minutes of sleep can leave you groggy and disoriented. So now, instead of hitting snooze, I start my day with a 10-minute yoga nidra session. It's a game changer—gentle, restorative, and energizing.

DARK THOUGHT EXPERIMENT

 Imagine a world where no one rests. People work endlessly, sacrificing sleep and downtime for the sake of productivity. Creativity vanishes because there's no space for daydreaming. Families grow distant because there's no time for shared meals or quiet evenings. Society becomes a machine, grinding itself into exhaustion until it collapses.

Now picture the opposite: a world where rest is sacred. Communities gather for afternoon siestas. Workplaces prioritize mental health by encouraging naps. Families spend evenings reconnecting, and individuals embrace rest as a vital part of their routine. Which world do you want to create? What can you do today to make rest a priority in your life?

INTERACTIVE EXERCISES

1. Watch Wild Behavior

Choose a documentary about mountain gorillas, orangutans, or another species that interests you. (Consider writing that "sparks your interest") Observe how they rest, interact, and conserve energy. Write down three takeaways and consider how you can apply them to your life.

2. Create a Restful Nest

Channel your inner orangutan by designing a space in your home specifically for rest. Add cozy textures, calming scents, and soft lighting. Use this space daily to relax and recharge.

3. Track Your Sleep

Keep a journal for one week, noting how many hours you sleep, how rested you feel, and what factors impact your sleep quality. Reflect on patterns and adjustments you can make.

4. Micro-Nap Experiment

Give yourself permission to rest with a 10–20-minute nap. If sleep feels elusive, try a soft eye-gaze practice, count your breaths, or simply close your eyes and let your body relax. Set a timer, settle in, and allow yourself to drift—perhaps into the valley of dreams. Notice how even a brief pause shifts your energy and mood.

EVIDENCE-BASED PRACTICES

Yoga Nidra

Studies show that yoga nidra reduces stress, improves sleep quality, and activates the parasympathetic nervous system, promoting deep relaxation.

The Neuroscience of Napping

Short naps (10–20 minutes) boost alertness and creativity, while longer naps (90 minutes) allow for a full sleep cycle, enhancing learning and problem-solving abilities.

Ditch the Snooze Button

Research reveals that fragmented sleep caused by snoozing can impair cognitive function and make you feel groggy. Replace snoozing with a calming wake-up practice like yoga nidra or deep breathing.

REFLECTION QUESTIONS

1. How does your relationship with rest compare to the natural rhythms of animals like apes or even your pets?

2. What societal pressures or personal beliefs prevent you from resting more fully?

3. What rituals or tools could you use to create more intentional rest in your daily life

CHEERING YOU ON: A REST REVOLUTION

If apes can nap in the midday sun and orangutans can build nests fit for royalty, then you—yes, you—deserve rest too. But let's be real: the world doesn't make it easy. You are living in a system designed to squeeze every last drop of energy from you. A culture that worships grind over grace, extraction over restoration. A machine that tells you your worth is measured in output, your value in exhaustion. It convinces you that stopping—just for a moment—is failure, that stillness is waste. And that's a lie.

Maybe you're exhausted but can't afford to stop. Maybe rest feels like a luxury someone else gets to have. I see you. I honor you. And I know that telling you to "just take a break" might sound naive, even infuriating. But hear this:

Rest is not a privilege. It is a right. And when a system denies you that right, resting becomes an act of defiance.

As Audre Lorde said, *"Caring for myself is not self-indulgence, it is self-preservation, and that is an act of political warfare."* Your rest is resistance. Your breath, your pause, your refusal to run yourself into the ground—these are small, quiet revolutions. And revolutions start somewhere. Even if it's just one deep breath. One moment of stillness. One reminder that you are more than what you produce.

So if you can, build your nest. Take up space. Let your body rest, even for a moment. And if you can't, if the world won't let you yet, know this: You deserve better.

We all do. And we will fight for a world where we don't just survive—we thrive.

Close your eyes, primate. You are not alone.

Chapter 4:
Sacred Grooming

"

"Touch comes before sight, before speech. It is the first language and the last, and it always tells the truth."
- Margaret Atwood

SUBVERSIVE ACT

Rediscover the transformative power of touch—both given and received—as a pathway to deeper connection, healing, and self-awareness.

INTRODUCTION: THE LANGUAGE OF CARE

 Touch is our first language. Before we can see or speak, we experience the world through touch. It tells us if we're safe, loved, or connected. Yet, in today's culture, touch has become a complicated, even fraught, subject.

We live in a world where touch is both desperately needed and heavily stigmatized. Studies show that Americans, on average, engage in far less physical touch than people in other cultures. One cross-cultural study found that French friends touched each other 110 times per hour while conversing in a café, compared to Americans, who touched just twice (Field, 2010). The COVID-19 pandemic only magnified this deficit. For months, many of us went without hugs, handshakes, or comforting pats on the back, leaving a void that was deeply felt but hard to name.

Touch, or the lack thereof, has profound effects on our well-being. Research has shown that touch deprivation can lead to increased anxiety, depression, and even physical pain. For infants, the consequences are even more severe: babies who are deprived of touch fail to thrive, showing delayed physical and emotional development (Hertenstein & Weiss, 2011). Without touch, what kind of culture do we create? One where isolation and disconnection reign.

At the same time, the complexity of touch cannot be ignored. In our world, the term "grooming" carries a dual meaning—one that reminds us how touch can be weaponized in abusive relationships. Acknowledging this reality is not about rejecting touch but reclaiming it in safe, consensual, and empowering ways.

This chapter is an invitation to heal our relationship with touch. Whether through self-grooming, meaningful connection with others, or reflecting on our cultural touch deficit, this is a call to action to reimagine and reclaim touch as a sacred, transformative act.

In our exploration of grooming, we've seen how our primate cousins use touch to bond, de-stress, and build community. But let's not tiptoe around the elephant in the room: sex. As Mae West famously quipped, "Sex is emotion in motion." It's high time we celebrate sex as a natural, joyous expression of our humanity.

While this chapter scratches the surface of grooming and physical touch, the rich tapestry of human sexuality deserves a deeper dive. So, consider this a tantalizing seed planting for future explorations, where we'll unabashedly delve into the delightful dance of desire. By embracing open conversations about all forms of touch—including the passionate and playful—we can foster a culture that celebrates connection in all its glorious forms.

PRIMATE CONNECTION: GROOMING AS SURVIVAL AND BONDING

 In the animal kingdom, grooming is far more than hygiene—it's a social glue. Among primates, grooming is the ultimate trust-building activity:

✓ **Chimpanzees:** Grooming is central to chimpanzee society. Allies groom each other to reinforce bonds, while rivals use grooming to repair relationships after conflicts. Yet, chimps also reveal the darker side of touch: infanticide and aggression show how physical contact can be weaponized for power.

✓ **Bonobos:** These peaceful primates use touch as a universal language of connection. Grooming, cuddling, and even playful physical contact maintain harmony and group cohesion.

✓ **Mountain Gorillas:** These gentle giants groom each other to relax, bond, and maintain social structure. Mothers groom their infants as an act of love, while troop members use grooming to build trust and reduce tension.

✓ **Humans Across Cultures:** In many cultures, touch is woven into daily rituals. Moroccan hammams provide spaces for communal care, while family hair-braiding in parts of Africa strengthens generational ties.

Grooming, in all its forms, is a language of connection, trust, and care. Even when it's just a casual touch on the arm or a shared laugh while applying sunscreen, it's a reminder that we're not alone.

THE SCIENCE OF TOUCH AND ITS ABSENCE

Touch is not just a social gesture—it's a biological necessity. Here's what happens when we experience safe, caring touch:

- **Oxytocin Release:** Known as the "bonding hormone," oxytocin fosters trust, reduces stress, and deepens social connections.

- **Stress Reduction:** Touch lowers cortisol levels, reducing feelings of anxiety and promoting relaxation.

- **Parasympathetic Activation:** Gentle touch activates the body's "rest and digest" mode, helping us feel calm and centered.

But what happens when touch is absent?

- **Touch Deprivation:** Chronic lack of touch has been linked to increased stress, depression, and even physical pain (Field, 2010). Studies show that children raised in touch-deprived environments—like orphanages—often experience delayed physical and emotional development (Hertenstein & Weiss, 2011).

- **Social Consequences:** Cultures that stigmatize touch often experience higher rates of loneliness and isolation. In the U.S., 46% of adults report feeling lonely, and touch deprivation is a contributing factor (Cigna, 2020).

Even self-touch can have profound effects. Research indicates that self-soothing gestures, like massaging your scalp or holding your own hand, can activate the same calming pathways as being touched by another person. Trauma-informed practices like self-massage or mindful grooming offer a way to reclaim the power of touch, even when connection with others feels too vulnerable.

A HUMAN STORY: THE CONDOR AND THE SOCK PUPPET

 When I was in grade school, I learned that California condors were on the brink of extinction. These magnificent birds, with their massive wingspans, were dwindling in numbers due to habitat destruction and poisoning. It broke my heart to think of a world without them.

But then I learned something remarkable. Conservationists discovered that captive baby condors had better survival rates when they were fed and groomed using sock puppets that mimicked their parents. These puppets provided the nurturing touch the chicks needed without creating dependency on humans. It was a strange but beautiful solution—proving that even simulated touch can save lives.

That story stayed with me. It reminded me of the fundamental truth that touch, in all its forms, is essential for survival—whether you're a condor, a chimp, or a human.

DARK THOUGHT EXPERIMENT

Imagine a world without touch. No one holds hands, hugs, or brushes another's hair. Relationships grow colder, trust erodes, and loneliness becomes the norm. People feel invisible, disconnected from themselves and others. What would this do to our mental health, our sense of community, our ability to thrive?

Now, imagine the opposite: a world where touch is sacred. Where every hug, every handshake, every gentle gesture carries meaning and care. What small acts of touch can you introduce into your life to bring this world into being?

INTERACTIVE EXERCISES

1. Self-Grooming as Ritual

Choose one grooming activity—like brushing your teeth or

washing your face—and turn it into a mindful practice. Focus on the sensations and think of this act as a way to honor your body.

2. Offer the Gift of Care

This week, offer someone an act of grooming care, like brushing a child's hair, massaging a partner's shoulders, or holding a friend's hand. Reflect on how this act deepens your connection.

3. Trauma-Informed Self-Touch

Practice a simple self-massage, like gently rubbing your temples or placing a hand on your heart. Notice how it feels to give yourself care, and reflect on any emotions that arise.

4. Recreate a Family Tradition

Think of a grooming tradition from your past—like combing a grandparent's hair or being bathed as a child. Recreate it, either for yourself or someone you love, and reflect on the emotions it stirs.

REFLECTION QUESTIONS

1. What messages did you receive about touch and grooming growing up? How have they shaped your relationship with self-care?

2. How can self-grooming become a more mindful and healing part of your daily routine?

3.   What barriers—emotional or societal—prevent you from experiencing safe, healing touch?

CONCLUSION

 Apes groom each other not just to clean fur, but to soothe, bond, and say, "I see you. I care for you." They don't overthink it. They don't ask if they're being too much. They reach out, and connection happens.

And yet, here we are—hairless primates, navigating a world that has convinced us to keep our hands to ourselves. Conditioned to believe that touch must be earned, justified, or feared. That loneliness is normal. That needing each other is weak. But let's call it what it is: a cruel, unnatural design. This world has robbed us of something sacred.

Somewhere along the way, capitalism, colonialism, and control-based culture severed us from one of the simplest, most instinctual ways we heal: through touch. It told us to be self-sufficient islands. To fear intimacy. To toughen up, detach, and get back to work. But our primate ancestors know better. And deep down, so do you.

Touch is not indulgence—it is survival. It is what makes us feel safe, known, and alive. It is what soothes the nervous system, dissolves stress, and reminds us that we belong.

So lean in. Not just to others, but to yourself. As Sanober Khan writes:

"lean in to kiss me
in all the places
where the ache
Is the most special."

Lean into that ache. Let it guide you, not shame you. Hold a hand. Stroke a cheek. Rest your head on a shoulder. Offer touch freely, without fear, without apology.

And if no one is there, then be there for yourself. Run your fingers through your own hair. Press your palm to your heart. Hold your own face as gently as you would a loved one's. Your nervous system won't know the difference—it just wants to feel safe, connected, held. We were never meant to live untouched. We were never meant to be this lonely. It's time to take back what has always been ours.

One touch at a time. One moment of connection. One reminder that you are, and have always been, worthy of love.

It ain't all doom when we're willing to groom!

Chapter 5:

Chimpanzee-ing Playfulness

"

"It is a happy talent to know how to play."
- Ralph Waldo Emerson

SUBVERSIVE ACT

Rediscover the joy of play—alone and with others—as a tool for healing, connection, and creativity.

INTRODUCTION: THE FORGOTTEN ART OF PLAY

 When I think about play, I'm reminded of a childhood spent wrestling with my brothers, running through the woods, and riding bikes until the sun dipped below the horizon. Play felt limitless, spontaneous, and essential. Looking back, I realize how lucky I was to have that freedom. As a queer kid, I found pockets of acceptance where I could play house or dolls—activities shunned by my family but encouraged by my neighbor's mom. Those moments of unstructured, joyful play were a refuge, a reminder of who I was before the world told me who I should be.

But somewhere along the way, play began to disappear. For many of us, it gets replaced by the seriousness of adulthood, the weight of responsibilities, and the rigid boundaries of what's deemed "acceptable." Add to this the challenges of a world that often feels unsafe—where children are no longer free to roam neighborhoods or explore the woods without close supervision—and it's no wonder that play has become an endangered species in human life.

Yet play is not a luxury; it's a necessity. It's how we learn, connect, and heal. For apes, play isn't just for the young; adults play too, using it as a way to bond, relieve tension, and sharpen social skills. If our primate relatives can teach us one thing about play, it's this: play is primal. It's not a frivolous pastime—it's a radical act of reclaiming joy and creativity in a world that often feels too serious.

PRIMATE CONNECTION: HOW APES PLAY

Play is woven into the lives of our closest relatives, and it's as diverse as it is fascinating.

✓ **Chimpanzees:** Chimpanzee play often mimics adult behaviors, like wrestling or mock-hunting, but without the stakes of survival. Young chimps chase each other, tumble, and engage in exaggerated gestures that signal, "This is just for fun!" Researchers have observed chimps using tools creatively during play, like rolling rocks or balancing sticks (Goodall, 1986).

✓ **Bonobos:** Known for their playful, affectionate nature, bonobos incorporate touch, laughter-like vocalizations, and even acrobatics into their play. Play is an essential tool for maintaining harmony in their groups.

✓ **Orangutans:** These gentle apes are often seen swinging through trees or splashing in water, demonstrating that play isn't just a juvenile activity—it's a lifelong way of engaging with the world.

✓ **Dogs and the Play Bow:** While not primates, dogs offer a perfect example of how animals communicate playfulness. The "play bow"—front legs lowered, tail wagging—is their way of saying, "Let's have fun!" Watching dogs navigate social dynamics in a dog park reveals the universality of play as a tool for connection.

THE NEUROSCIENCE OF PLAY: WHAT HAPPENS IN OUR BRAINS

When we play, our brains light up. Play activates the prefrontal cortex, stimulating creativity, problem-solving, and emotional regulation. Here's how play impacts our minds and bodies:

- **Dopamine Release:** Play triggers the release of dopamine, the "feel-good" neurotransmitter that enhances mood and motivation.

- **Social Bonding:** Oxytocin, the "bonding hormone," is often released during social play, strengthening connections and trust between participants.

- **Stress Reduction:** Play reduces cortisol levels, helping to alleviate stress and anxiety.

- **Neuroplasticity:** Play promotes brain flexibility by encouraging new ways of thinking and problem-solving. This is why play is so vital for both children's development and adult creativity.

But there's more. Trauma-informed research shows that play can be a pathway to healing. For those who have experienced trauma, play offers a low-stakes, joyful way to rebuild trust, regulate emotions, and reconnect with the body.

A HUMAN STORY: REDISCOVERING PLAY IN ADULTHOOD

After years of feeling disconnected from joy, I decided to try something simple: blowing bubbles. It sounds ridiculous, I know. But standing in my backyard, watching those iridescent spheres float into the air, something shifted. I felt lighter, freer, as if I'd tapped into a part of myself I hadn't accessed in years.

That small act of play led me to explore more. I started tossing a frisbee with friends, rolling down grassy hills, and even trying adult dodgeball leagues. Each activity brought laughter, connection, and a sense of being fully alive.

But I also had to confront my discomfort with play—especially in a world that often views adult playfulness as immature. Reclaiming play wasn't just about fun; it was an act of defiance against a culture that equates seriousness with worth.

DARK THOUGHT EXPERIMENT

Imagine a world without play. Children are confined to desks, never running or exploring. Adults move through life like machines, never laughing, never playing. Creativity dies, relationships become transactional, and joy disappears.

Now imagine the opposite: a world where play is woven into the fabric of life. Adults climb trees, children invent imaginary worlds, and workplaces encourage creativity and playfulness. How would this world feel? What can you do to make it a reality in your own life?

INTERACTIVE EXERCISES

1. Play Inventory

Reflect on your favorite childhood games or activities. Write down three that brought you joy. Then, brainstorm how you could adapt these for your adult life.

2. Solo Play Exploration

Set aside 30 minutes to play by yourself. Build with LEGO, color in a book, or dance like nobody's watching. Notice how it feels to let go of judgment and simply enjoy.

3. Social Play Challenge

Organize a playful activity with friends or family. This could be as simple as a game of tag, a scavenger hunt, or a group craft project. Reflect on how it strengthens your bonds.

4. Animal Observation

Visit a playground, dog park, or zoo and watch how animals—human or otherwise—play. Notice their body language, the way they signal trust, set boundaries, and express joy. See how movement, curiosity, and connection shape their interactions. What lessons can you take from their natural rhythms, and how might you invite more of that ease into your own life?

EVIDENCE-BASED PRACTICES

1. Play Therapy

Originally designed for children, play therapy has been shown to help adults process trauma and reconnect with joy in a safe, structured way.

2. Movement Play

Activities like dance, yoga, or free-form movement can reduce stress and boost creativity by engaging the body in playful ways.

3. Laughter Yoga

Combining deep breathing with intentional laughter, this practice has been shown to reduce stress and improve mood.

REFLECTION QUESTIONS

1. What role did play have in your childhood? How has that changed in adulthood?

2. What societal pressures or personal beliefs make it hard for you to embrace play?

3. How can you create space for more play in your life—both alone and with others?

CONCLUSION

"Most adults make adulthood seem like a disease that is caused by a deficiency of playfulness."

— Mokokoma Mokhonoana

And what a sickness it is. A plague of overwork, seriousness, and self-denial. A world that convinces us that play is for children, that joy must be earned, and that if we're not exhausted, we're not doing enough.

But let's be honest—who does that serve?

Certainly not you. Not your nervous system. Not your spirit. It serves the system that wants you compliant, producing, too tired to imagine anything different. It serves a culture that worships work and calls anything joyful frivolous. It serves those who want you to forget that play is not a distraction—it is your birthright.

And yet here you are—maybe feeling the spark, maybe skeptical, maybe wondering where play fits into your life.

Oh, but it does. It must.

Because play is how we reconnect—to ourselves, to each other, to a world beyond deadlines and survival mode. Play is how we rebel.

So go back to the mirror. Yes, again. Look at yourself. But this time, stick out your tongue. Make a ridiculous face. Wiggle your eyebrows. Dance like a fool. Let yourself be stupid, awkward, joyful. If your reflection judges you, laugh at it. That voice in your head? The one telling you to grow up? Tell it to go take a nap.

Because growing up was never supposed to mean giving up joy.

So what's it going to be? Another day defined merely by productivity? Another year waiting for permission to play? Or will you break the cycle and take back what was stolen from you? Go. Run, laugh, tumble, and create.

Play like your life depends on it—because it does.

Because life isn't meant to be endured—it's meant to be played.

Chapter 6:

Banana Peels of Failure

"

"Perfection is the thief of joy."
- Theodore Roosevelt

SUBVERSIVE ACT

Embrace failure as a pathway to growth, laughter, and resilience, reframing setbacks as stepping stones to self-discovery.

INTRODUCTION: SLIPPING ON THE PEEL

 When I was a kid, I thought failure was the worst thing that could happen. I wanted to be perfect—flawless at school, sports, and even how I played with my toys. But perfectionism didn't bring joy. It brought anxiety, avoidance, and an overwhelming fear of making mistakes. Now, in my mid-50s, I've let go of perfection and adopted a mantra: *preciousness over precision*. Life isn't about getting everything right; it's about finding the beauty in the messy, imperfect process.

Failure, I've learned, isn't the enemy—it's the teacher. And when we avoid failure, we also avoid growth, connection, and joy. This fear holds us back from big moments, like asking someone on a date, and even small ones, like trying a new recipe or starting a conversation.

In this chapter, we'll explore how to shift our perspective on failure, drawing inspiration from our primate relatives, neuroscience, and personal stories. If laughter and play are tools for healing, failure is the sharpening stone. Let's learn how to slip, fall, and rise stronger than ever.

PRIMATE CONNECTION: LEARNING THROUGH FAILURE

 In the Disney documentary *Chimpanzee*, a young chimp repeatedly hits their hand with a rock while trying to crack open a nut. Again and again, they fumble, miss the mark, and hit their fingers. But failure doesn't stop them—it teaches them. Eventually, after countless tries, they master the skill. Watching this unfold reminded me that growth takes time, patience, and a whole lot of missteps.

- ✓ **Chimpanzees:** Tool use in chimps is a testament to persistence. Whether it's cracking nuts or fishing for termites, these skills require repeated failure to master (Goodall, 1986). Young chimps often watch adults before trying for themselves, imitating movements that initially seem clumsy but gradually become precise.

- ✓ **Bonobos:** In bonobo play, failure is met with laughter and encouragement. A bonobo might tumble during a game of chase or misjudge a jump, but they bounce back with enthusiasm, often trying again immediately.

- ✓ **Orangutans:** Orangutans learning to build nests often fail to secure branches properly, causing their sleeping structures to collapse. These failures don't deter them—they refine their methods with each attempt, eventually creating intricate, stable nests (Fruth & Hohmann, 1996).

Failure in the animal kingdom isn't just tolerated—it's essential. It's how young primates develop problem-solving skills, resilience, and confidence.

THE NEUROSCIENCE OF FAILURE: A GROWTH OPPORTUNITY

Failure activates specific pathways in the brain, creating opportunities for growth and adaptation:

- **Neuroplasticity:** When we make mistakes, our brains form new neural connections to address what went wrong. This process strengthens learning and helps us adapt to future challenges (Dweck, 2006).

- **Dopamine Reward System:** Overcoming failure triggers dopamine release, reinforcing resilience and motivation. The brain rewards effort and persistence, even when success isn't immediate.

- **Fear Response vs. Curiosity:** Perfectionism often stems from fear—fear of rejection, judgment, or inadequacy. Research shows that shifting from a fear-based mindset to a curious one (e.g., "What can I learn from this?") changes how the brain processes failure, making it less emotionally charged (Center for Compassion and Altruism Research and Education, 2019).

A HUMAN STORY: TOOLS TAKE TIME

Watching that young chimp struggle to crack open a nut reminded me of my own clumsy attempts at learning. Writing this book, for example, has been a process of trial and error. Entire sections have been rewritten, scrapped, or reimagined. Every chapter feels like its own version of that chimp with a rock, fumbling toward something that works.

But it's not just big projects like books or tools. Failure touches every part of our lives—dating, friendships, work, and even self-care. I've avoided asking someone out because I feared rejection. I've hesitated to admit when I needed help because I didn't want to seem weak. But every time I've pushed past that fear, I've found something unexpected: connection, growth, and a deeper sense of self.

Failure isn't just about persistence—it's about being brave enough to try in the first place.

DARK THOUGHT EXPERIMENT

Imagine a world where failure is forbidden. People only attempt what they're certain they can do perfectly. Creativity disappears, innovation halts, and society stagnates. Children stop experimenting, adults stick to what's familiar, and relationships remain shallow because no one dares to be vulnerable.

Now imagine the opposite: a world where failure is celebrated. Children are encouraged to take risks, workplaces reward experimentation, and people laugh at their mistakes instead of hiding them. How would this world feel? What can you do today to create it in your own life?

INTERACTIVE EXERCISES

1.   Reframe a Recent Failure

Think about a recent failure—something that felt discouraging or embarrassing. Write down three things you learned from the experience. How did it help you grow?

2. The Fail Forward Journal

Start a journal where you document your failures. For each one, note what went wrong, what you learned, and how you can approach it differently next time.

3. Try Something New

Pick an activity you've always wanted to try but avoided because of fear of failure—dancing, painting, cooking, or public speaking. Commit to trying it this week, and focus on the joy of the process rather than the outcome.

4. Role Models of Resilience

Research someone you admire who has faced significant failures. Write about how their perseverance inspires you and what lessons you can apply to your own life.

EVIDENCE-BASED PRACTICES

Adopt a Growth Mindset

Dr. Carol Dweck's research highlights the importance of viewing challenges as opportunities. Practice telling yourself, "I can learn from this," instead of, "I can't do this."

2. Mindfulness and Self-Compassion

Mindfulness can help you detach from the emotional sting of failure. Pair it with self-compassion practices like Dr. Kristin Neff's Self-Compassion Break: acknowledge the pain, recognize that failure is universal, and offer yourself kindness.

3. Normalize Mistakes

Share your failures with a friend or loved one. Research shows that openly discussing mistakes reduces their emotional impact and fosters a sense of shared humanity (Brown, 2012).

REFLECTION QUESTIONS

1. How has perfectionism influenced your decisions? What has it kept you from trying?

2. What can you learn from your recent failures, and how can you apply those lessons?

3. How can you cultivate a growth mindset in your daily life, seeing challenges as opportunities rather than obstacles?

CONCLUSION

 Perfectionism is a thief. It robs us of joy, creativity, and the freedom to be human. We live in a culture obsessed with flawless execution, with getting it right the first time, as if failure is something to fear rather than embrace. But what if we looked at the natural world—at our fellow great apes—for guidance?

Chimpanzees don't quit when they can't crack a nut on the first try. They fumble, they adjust, they keep at it—sometimes for hours, sometimes for years—until they master the skill. Orangutans watch, experiment, and learn through play, embracing the trial-and-error process that makes them some of the most intelligent primates. Even gorillas, who rarely use tools, adapt and innovate when needed, showing us that learning is a lifelong process.

> *"Ring the bells that still can ring*
> *Forget your perfect offering*
> *There is a crack in everything*
> *That's how the light gets in."*
> —Leonard Cohen

Nature doesn't demand perfection; it demands persistence. Evolution itself is failure refined over time.

The cracks, the mistakes, the imperfect offerings—these are where growth happens, where the light gets in.

So let's stop treating failure as something shameful. Let's aim for preciousness over precision, for curiosity over control. The revolution starts when we stop fearing failure and start celebrating it—when we show up, fumble, and try again. Crack open your expectations and let the light in.

Chapter 7:

Unlearning the
Jungle Rules

"

> *"The most subversive thing you can do is to actually
> believe in a better future—and act as if it's possible."*
> **- Angela Davis**

SUBVERSIVE ACT

Challenge societal norms that perpetuate oppression, rewrite the rules that keep us silent, and dare to imagine a new path for humanity's evolution.

INTRODUCTION: BEYOND HOMO SAPIENS

 In this chapter—and throughout the book—I use *Jungle Rules* not to disrespect the laws of nature, but to highlight how human societal norms often masquerade as civility while running on domination, scarcity, and survival instincts we barely acknowledge.

Humanity is teetering on the edge of a critical decision. On one side lies extinction—a descent into fear, division, and endless cycles of conflict. On the other lies something more profound than mere survival: the possibility of evolution. Not just an evolution of technology or intellect, but an evolution of heart—a shift toward becoming something radically different.

What if we're on the cusp of moving beyond Homo sapiens? What if our future lies in becoming Homo cordis—beings led by empathy and compassion—or Homo animus, in harmony with the web of life and driven by connection rather than dominance? Evolution does not demand perfection, but it does demand adaptation. To take this step, we must confront the jungle rules that have held us captive for centuries:

- Stay quiet.
- Conform.
- Power belongs to the ruthless.

These rules have brought us to the brink of disaster. They have silenced voices, broken spirits, and allowed oppression to flourish. But rules are not immutable—they can be rewritten. And the only way forward is to challenge the very foundation of what we've been told is normal.

PRIMATE CONNECTION: THE POWER OF KINDNESS IN BONOBO SOCIETIES

 Our closest relatives—chimpanzees and bonobos—offer two very different models for navigating power and conflict. Understanding their behaviors helps us reflect on the choices humanity faces when confronting societal challenges.

✓ **Chimpanzees:** The Aggressive Hierarchy

Chimpanzee societies are often hierarchical and male-dominated, with power maintained through aggression and intimidation. Alphas assert control through physical dominance, but their power isn't absolute. Alliances between lower-ranking males can overthrow an alpha, highlighting the potential for collective action even in violent systems. Yet, chimpanzees are also capable of tenderness and care, particularly toward their young and close allies (Goodall, 1986).

However, violence is a stark reality. Chimps have been observed engaging in brutal acts, including infanticide and lethal territorial disputes. This darker side of chimpanzee behavior mirrors the cycles of violence we see in human societies when power is hoarded and fear drives decisions.

✓ **Bonobos:** The Gentle Matriarchy

Bonobos present a striking contrast. Their matriarchal societies prioritize cooperation, connection, and conflict resolution through touch and play. When tensions arise, bonobos diffuse them through grooming, laughter, or even sexual behavior, which serves as a tool for maintaining harmony and reducing aggression (De Waal, 1997).

Bonobos teach us that gentleness isn't weakness—it's a survival strategy. Their societies thrive not because they avoid conflict but because they approach it with creativity and compassion, valuing the collective good over individual dominance.

These two models—aggressive dominance versus cooperative harmony—exist on a spectrum. Humanity, like our primate relatives, carries the potential for both. The question is: which approach will we choose? And more importantly, can we find a balance between strength and compassion as we confront our own societal woes?

THE COST OF THE JUNGLE RULES: A WORLD AT RISK

The rules of dominance, fear, and silence are not abstract concepts—they manifest in the very real challenges we face today:

- **LGBTQ+ Rights:** Trans youth and the LGBTQ+ community are under attack, with over 500 anti-LGBTQ+ bills introduced in 2023 alone. These laws strip away rights and safety, forcing many to live in fear and silence (Human Rights Campaign, 2023).

- **Economic Inequality:** The top 1% holds more wealth than the bottom 90% combined, while millions struggle to access basic needs like housing and healthcare (World Inequality Report, 2022).

- **Mental Health Crisis:** Marginalized communities face skyrocketing rates of anxiety and depression. Trans youth are four times more likely to attempt suicide than their cisgender peers (The Trevor Project, 2023).

- **Environmental Collapse:** The planet's ecosystems are unraveling due to deforestation, climate change, and biodiversity loss, driven by systems that prioritize profit over sustainability.

- **The Dismantling of DEI:** DEI (Diversity, Equity, Inclusion) programs are not failing—they're being sabotaged. While corporations like Amazon, Google, and Walmart quietly dismantle diversity programs under political pressure, nearly 60% of U.S. workers still support them (Loudenback, Business Insider, 2024). The real question isn't whether DEI works, but who benefits from stopping it.

These challenges are symptoms of a deeper sickness: the unchecked dominance of fear, greed, and exclusion. The jungle rules aren't working—they're killing us.

A HUMAN STORY: WRESTLING WITH THE RULES

Growing up, I absorbed the jungle rule that said, "Stay quiet. Don't make waves. Don't let anyone see you struggle." Playing house with dolls at my neighbor's house felt like freedom, but it was also a secret—something I couldn't share without risking ridicule. The unspoken rules of my family and society taught me to hide who I was.

For years, I internalized those rules. I stayed silent when I wanted to speak up, hid parts of myself to avoid rejection, and let fear guide my choices. That silence came at a cost. I lived with a constant sense of self-loathing, which seeped into my relationships, my work, and even my health. Chronic stress and sleepless nights became my normal.

But something shifted. Therapy helped me confront the shame I didn't even realize I carried. Yoga taught me to sit with discomfort and reconnect with my body. And psychedelics opened doors I hadn't known existed, showing me a version of myself beyond the rules I'd been living by.

Even now, the work isn't done. Writing this book is part of that ongoing process—my way of challenging the rules that kept me small for so long. If there's one thing I've learned, it's this: the jungle rules can be rewritten.

DARK THOUGHT EXPERIMENT

Imagine a world where the jungle rules dominate. Silence replaces conversation, fear replaces compassion, and progress grinds to a halt. What happens to love, creativity, and freedom in such a world?

Now imagine a world where the rules are rewritten. Empathy replaces fear, equity dismantles hierarchies, and safety becomes a right, not a privilege. What small acts can you take today to move us closer to this vision?

INTERACTIVE EXERCISES

1. Rewrite Your Rules

Identify a rule you've internalized, like "Don't speak up" or "Don't take risks." Rewrite it into something empowering, like "My voice matters" or "Failure is growth."

2. Balance Strength and Compassion

Reflect on a recent conflict in your life. Did you approach it with dominance or gentleness? Consider how you might balance the two in future situations.

3. Collective Imagination

Gather a group of friends or colleagues and brainstorm ways to challenge harmful norms in your community. What does a better future look like, and how can you work toward it together?

EVIDENCE-BASED PRACTICES

Mindful Resistance

Use mindfulness to ground yourself when fear or doubt arises. Focused breathing can help you stay present and courageous in the face of challenges.

Compassion Training

Engage in practices like loving-kindness meditation to strengthen your capacity for empathy and connection.

Trauma-Informed Advocacy

Recognize that many people you engage with may carry trauma. Approach your activism with sensitivity and a commitment to centering marginalized voices.

REFLECTION QUESTIONS

1. What jungle rules have shaped your life, and how can you begin to unlearn them?

2. How can you challenge the norms that perpetuate oppression in your community or workplace?

3. What does an evolved humanity look like to you, and how can you embody that vision today?

CONCLUSION: EVOLVING BEYOND THE RULES

 The laws of the human jungle have never truly served us. They were written by those who sought to dominate, not those who sought to thrive. But here's the truth: We are not bound by them. Evolution demands change, and we are the architects of what comes next.

In gorilla troops, power shifts when a dominant silverback weakens or falls. The transition is rarely smooth—rivalries flare, tensions rise—but ultimately, a new leader emerges. And when that leader proves they can protect and provide, the troop adapts. They do not cling to a failing system out of nostalgia or fear; they move forward because survival depends on it.

We are preparing for such a transition. The leaders and systems that once ruled over us—built on unchecked power, oppression, and exclusion—are faltering. Some cling desperately to control, but their time is up. The question is: Will we continue to obey the old rules, the ones designed to serve only a privileged few, or will we rewrite them to create a future where all can thrive?

"I don't say women's rights—I say the constitutional principle of the equal citizenship stature of men and women."

—Ruth Bader Ginsburg

Justice is not a privilege; it's a principle. Equality is not a debate; it's a demand. The structures that shape our world today are not natural; they are manufactured, upheld, and long overdue for dismantling. To move forward, we must challenge every system that tells us we are separate, that we must compete to survive, that some lives are worth more than others.

But rewriting the rules is not just about dismantling oppression—it is about defining what comes next. What will replace these outdated systems? What moral code will guide us forward? Awareness without action is empty. Community without accountability is fragile. Faith without courage is meaningless.

This is not about small reforms; this is about rewriting the human story. And that story is being written now—by those who refuse to stay silent, who dare to reimagine what it means to be human.

So the question remains: Will you cling to the old rules, or will you help write the new ones?

Chapter 8:
Troop Mentality Over Me-First Thinking

"

> "We are here to awaken from the illusion of our separateness."
>
> — **Thich Nhat Hanh**

SUBVERSIVE ACT

Embrace interdependence and prioritize collective well-being over individual gain. Challenge the glorification of independence by cultivating community, connection, and accountability, especially across lines of privilege and power.

INTRODUCTION: INTERDEPENDENCE AS STRENGTH

 I grew up in rural Pennsylvania, where winters were harsh, and survival often meant relying on your neighbors. If snow blocked the driveway, the family down the road plowed it. When summer came, we hauled hay for their dairy cows. It was unspoken, but deeply understood: we belonged to each other. Later, in Japan, I experienced another form of interdependence. The collectivism there was different but just as profound—rooted in the principle that if you take care of the group, your own needs will be met.

Yet, in modern America, we are immersed in a culture that idolizes independence. The myth of the self-made individual casts relationships as optional and community as secondary. But this mindset ignores a fundamental truth: **we were never meant to go it alone**.

Interdependence demands more than collaboration—it demands accountability. For those of us with privilege, especially white people, this means recognizing how systemic inequality has undermined the very idea of collective care. White fragility—the discomfort or defensiveness white people often feel when confronted with racial inequity—keeps us from building true community. If we genuinely believe "we belong to each other," we must dismantle the systems and beliefs that perpetuate division.

PRIMATE CONNECTION: TROOP MENTALITY IN ACTION

Our closest primate relatives live by interdependence, and their survival depends on it.

✓ **Chimpanzees:** In chimp societies, alliances are critical. Chimpanzees groom each other to build trust and form bonds that help them navigate power dynamics. These alliances are not just about survival but about shared responsibility and mutual benefit (Goodall, 1986).

✓ **Bonobos:** Bonobos excel in collaboration, resolving conflicts through touch, play, and shared resources. Their societies demonstrate that harmony can be a powerful survival strategy (De Waal, 1997).

✓ **Gorillas:** Mountain gorillas live in tight family groups, with the silverback often protecting the troop at great personal risk. Their collective strength lies in their shared sense of responsibility.

Humans evolved in similar ways, thriving in small, cooperative communities. Yet, modern society often replaces collective care with individualism. To reclaim our humanity, we must rebuild the "troop mentality"—a sense of belonging rooted in mutual accountability.

THE COST OF HYPER-INDIVIDUALISM AND PRIVILEGE

Hyper-individualism has fractured our communities, while systemic privilege—especially white privilege—has enabled some to live at the expense of others. Together, they create a toxic cycle of separation:

- **Loneliness Epidemic:** Nearly half of U.S. adults report feeling lonely, and loneliness is as harmful to health as smoking 15 cigarettes a day (Holt-Lunstad, 2015).

- **Mental Health Crisis:** Marginalized groups, particularly people of color and LGBTQ+ individuals, face higher rates of anxiety and depression due to systemic oppression (CDC, 2021).

- **White Fragility's Role:** White people's discomfort with conversations about privilege often stifles progress toward equity. Avoidance perpetuates inequality, isolating individuals and communities from genuine connection (DiAngelo, 2018).

- **Community Breakdown:** The decline of communal spaces and mutual aid has left many feeling disconnected and unsupported.

True interdependence requires addressing these challenges head-on. It means asking hard questions: How have I benefited from systems of oppression? What role can I play in dismantling them?

A HUMAN STORY: LEARNING TO BELONG

 By now, you know I'm proud to have grown up in the Keystone State—especially when I reflect on how my small-town upbringing shaped my understanding of community and survival. Whether it was shoveling snow or sharing meals, our lives were intertwined. But it wasn't until much later, living in Japan, that I fully grasped the depth of interdependence. There, the phrase "wa" (harmony) guided everything, from family gatherings to work culture.

In self-publishing this book, I know I'm bound to get feedback about where my blind spots are and the shortcomings of my perspective. That's part of the deal. My work is far from done—and that, in itself, is my hope for humanity: that each of us finds a place to do our work, to strengthen the troop we all belong to.

And yet, I can't ignore the ways privilege has shaped my understanding of belonging. As a white person, I was often shielded from the systemic inequities others faced. It took years—and a lot of unlearning—to see that interdependence isn't just about relying on others; it's about making sure everyone belongs, not just those who look or live like me.

That process hasn't been easy, and it never really ends. Acknowledging my privilege meant confronting the ways I'd been complicit in systems that harm others. It meant sitting with discomfort, listening more than speaking, and committing to ongoing learning. But it also meant discovering a deeper, richer sense of connection—one rooted in accountability and shared humanity. And that's why this book isn't meant to be the final word—it's my invitation. An invitation to question, to push back, to offer your own perspectives.

Because if we're really serious about evolving, we can't just accept the story we've been handed. We have to write a new one—together.

DARK THOUGHT EXPERIMENT

 Imagine a world where the myth of independence has reached its extreme—a society where "every man for himself" is the law of the land. Neighbors no longer greet each other, let alone offer help. Schools are privatized and accessible only to the wealthy. Healthcare is a luxury, not a right. Roads are riddled with potholes because no one wants to pay taxes to fix them. In this world, kindness is seen as weakness, and asking for help is a sign of failure.

Without a sense of collective responsibility, safety nets disappear. Families grow isolated, unable to rely on the support of extended networks. The elderly are left to age alone, without visitors or caregivers. Children grow up without the experience of community, and loneliness becomes an inherited condition. Cities become battlegrounds of competition, with everyone hoarding resources and protecting what little they have. Trust is a relic of the past, and fear becomes the default state of being.

Now consider the personal toll. Studies have shown that chronic loneliness increases the risk of premature death by 26%—comparable to the health risks of smoking or obesity (Holt-Lunstad, 2015). Social isolation not only weakens mental health, leading to higher rates of depression and anxiety, but also corrodes the immune system, leaving individuals more vulnerable to illness. Substance abuse rates skyrocket as people seek solace in fleeting numbing agents rather than meaningful connection.

Imagine living in this world. What would it feel like to have no one to turn to, no one to celebrate your successes or mourn your losses? How would it feel to walk through life knowing you are truly on your own?

Now shift your perspective. Imagine a world where belonging is the foundation of life. Picture communities where people pool resources, support one another through hardships, and celebrate each other's milestones. Imagine neighborhoods where everyone knows each other's names and children feel safe playing in the streets.

In this world, healthcare is a shared priority, and education is seen as a communal investment in the future. Elders are surrounded by care and companionship, their wisdom woven into the fabric of the community. Families, whether chosen or biological, thrive in a network of mutual support. People feel seen, valued, and connected.

In this world, the phrase "we belong to each other" is more than an ideal—it is a way of life. The air is filled with laughter, the streets with trust, and the homes with love. Every small act of care—plowing a neighbor's driveway, carrying hay for their cows, cooking a meal for a sick friend—becomes a thread in the tapestry of belonging.

What steps can you take today to help build this world? How can you challenge the myths of individualism and isolation, and instead foster interdependence in your own life and community?

INTERACTIVE EXERCISES

1.   Acknowledge Privilege

Write a list of privileges you hold—racial, socioeconomic, gender, or otherwise. Reflect on how these privileges have shaped your life and how you can use them to support others.

2. Troop Care Challenge

Identify three ways you can support your community this week—whether it's checking in on a neighbor, volunteering, or donating to a cause. Reflect on how these actions strengthen your sense of connection.

3. Learn and Listen

Choose a book, podcast, or workshop on racial equity or systemic oppression. Commit to listening and learning without defensiveness, and reflect on how these insights can inform your actions.

4. Circle Back to the Troop

Reach out to someone you've lost touch with—a friend, family member, or colleague. Rekindle the connection and reflect on how it feels to rebuild those bonds.

EVIDENCE-BASED PRACTICES

Community Health

Research shows that strong social ties improve mental health, reduce stress, and increase longevity. Investing in relationships is not just emotional—it's biological (Holt-Lunstad, 2015).

Accountability Practices

Engage in racial equity training or join local groups working toward social justice. Accountability strengthens community bonds and fosters a sense of shared purpose.

Mindful Interbeing

Inspired by Thich Nhat Hanh's teachings, practice mindfulness with an emphasis on connection. During meditation, reflect on the ways your life is intertwined with others'.

REFLECTION QUESTIONS

1. How has hyper-individualism shaped your life, and what steps can you take to unlearn it?

2. How can you hold yourself accountable for addressing privilege in your relationships and community?

3. What does interdependence look like in your daily life, and how can you nurture it further?

CONCLUSION: FROM ME TO WE

Interdependence isn't a weakness—it's a revolutionary act. It defies the myth of self-reliance, dismantles the illusion of privilege, and calls us to embrace a deeper truth: *we belong to each other.*

In the wild, even the most powerful apes do not survive alone. Studies show that chimpanzees and gorillas not only form alliances within their own species but also forge lifelong friendships across species boundaries. If our primate cousins understand the strength of connection, why do we resist it?

Thich Nhat Hanh's teachings on Interbeing remind us that nothing exists in isolation—our survival, our joy, and even our suffering are deeply intertwined. Yet, we live in a country that exalts Independence as its highest virtue. Imagine instead a nation that graduates from celebrating self-reliance to honoring Interdependence, a day when we gather not to declare separation, but to affirm that our liberation is bound together.

Like bonobos who use touch to resolve conflict and chimps who protect their allies for life, we too have the capacity to rewrite what it means to belong. But this isn't passive work—it's active, radical, and sometimes deeply uncomfortable. It means unlearning, listening, and showing up, especially when it's inconvenient.

Let's dare to build a world where Interdependence is our strength, not our shame—a world where no one is left behind, and where the ties that bind us are stronger than the forces that seek to divide us.

Chapter 9:

Primate Picks: Conscious Consumption

"

"*The most common way people give up their power is by thinking they don't have any.*"
                                                        - Alice Walker

SUBVERSIVE ACT

Make intentional choices about what you consume—whether it's food, media, or material goods—while finding ways to reuse, repurpose, and reduce waste.

INTRODUCTION: THE POWER OF INTENTIONAL CHOICES

 We live in a world of excess. In our modern jungles, it's easy to accumulate more than we need—more stuff, more food, more screen time, and, often, more guilt about all of it. But what if we reframed consumption not as a burden but as an opportunity? What if each choice about what we bring into our lives became a declaration of our values?

In my neighborhood, nearly every block has a little box where people leave "free items" for others to take. Old toys, kitchenware, clothes—it's like a mini treasure hunt. We also love using the OfferUp app, swapping items with strangers instead of buying new. My personal favorite is the network of tiny libraries scattered throughout our city. These little wooden boxes are filled with books, waiting to be read and passed on.

I'm also an animist, which means I believe everything—living or not—has a sacred essence. For me, it's painful to see a resource wasted. Like the scene in Toy Story 3 where Andy gives away his childhood toys to a young girl, I find joy in seeing items given a second life. They carry stories, histories, and purpose beyond their original use.

Still, the goal here isn't to wallow in guilt or shame. Instead, it's to recognize that consumption isn't just about taking—it's also about sharing, repurposing, and honoring the life cycle of the things we use. And here's the thing: we can learn a lot about this from our primate cousins.

PRIMATE CONNECTION: CONSUMING WITH CARE IN NATURE

 Primates in the wild and captivity demonstrate remarkable resourcefulness. Their behaviors highlight how animals can interact with their environment without overexploiting it.

✓ Chimpanzees: Strategic Foragers

In the wild, chimpanzees are mindful foragers. They select ripe fruit and rotate feeding areas to avoid overharvesting a single resource, allowing plants to regenerate (Wrangham, 2009). This strategy ensures the survival of their ecosystem while meeting their dietary needs.

✓ Bonobos: Cooperative Sharing

Bonobos often share food, especially when it's plentiful. Rather than hoard resources, they distribute them among their troop, reducing waste and fostering community (De Waal, 1997).

✓ Orangutans: Minimalists of the Canopy

Orangutans, who spend most of their time in the treetops, use leaves and branches to create nests, umbrellas, and even tools. Their resource use is efficient and low-impact, leaving their habitat intact (van Schaik, 2004).

✓ Captive Gorillas: Repurposing for Enrichment

In zoos, gorillas often repurpose objects provided for enrichment. Cardboard boxes become puzzle feeders, burlap sacks transform into hammocks, and sticks are used for play or problem-solving. This adaptability mirrors the creativity we need to repurpose resources in our human lives.

A PRIMAL PLAYFULNESS WITH CONSUMPTION

In the natural world, survival depends on resourcefulness. Watching animals engage with their environment can inspire us to think outside the box:

- Chimpanzees in the wild use leaves as sponges to collect water.
- Elephants use branches as fly swatters and tools to dig for water.
- Even crows, known for their intelligence, create tools to access food.

This kind of creativity invites us to ask: What would happen if we approached our consumption with the same curiosity and playfulness? Could an old

T-shirt become a tote bag? Could a broken chair be transformed into a shelf? The possibilities are endless when we allow ourselves to imagine.

THE COST OF OVERCONSUMPTION

Overconsumption isn't just a personal problem; it's a planetary one. Here's the cost of our collective excess:

- ✓ **Waste:** The average American generates over 4 pounds of trash per day, adding up to nearly 300 million tons annually (EPA, 2020). Much of this waste ends up in landfills or oceans, harming ecosystems and wildlife.

- ✓ **Climate Impact:** The production, transportation, and disposal of goods contribute significantly to carbon emissions, accelerating climate change (IPCC, 2021).

- ✓ **Resource Depletion:** Overextraction of resources like water, minerals, and timber is driving species extinction and habitat loss at alarming rates.

But here's the hopeful part: small, intentional changes can make a big difference.

THE ROLE OF MEDIA CONSUMPTION

It's not just material goods we consume—it's also information. In our digital age, over-consuming media can leave us just as drained as hoarding physical objects. Doomscrolling, binge-watching, and constant notifications can overwhelm our brains, leaving little room for creativity or connection.

Interactive exercise:

- For one week, track your media habits. How much time do you spend scrolling social media, reading the news, or watching TV? How do these activities make you feel afterward? What could you replace them with to feel more inspired or centered?

A HUMAN STORY: THE JOY OF GIVING THINGS A SECOND LIFE

In my household, we have too many things. Over the years, I've tried to shift my mindset from "how can I get rid of this?" to "how can I give this a second life?" That shift has changed everything.

My neighborhood is a hub for sharing. There's the "free items" box down the street, where I've both found treasures and passed them along. The mini library boxes in our city are a constant reminder of how stories—and even physical objects like books—connect us. And I'll never forget the thrill of watching my neighbor's child ride the old bike we gave them, their joy proving that things can have multiple lifetimes.

These small acts of conscious consumption have brought not only practical benefits but also emotional ones. Sharing creates connections. Repurposing brings creativity. And most importantly, it reminds me that we're all part of a larger cycle.

DARK THOUGHT EXPERIMENT

Imagine a world where consumption knows no bounds. Landfills overflow with discarded goods. Forests are stripped bare for paper and furniture. Oceans are filled with plastic, choking marine life. In this world, people buy more and more but feel less and less fulfilled. Things are consumed and discarded without thought, leaving a trail of destruction behind.

Now imagine the opposite: a world where consumption is intentional. Items are shared, repaired, and reused. Communities thrive on swapping and lending rather than buying new. Trash becomes treasure, and waste is nearly eliminated. What kind of person would you need to be to help build this world?

INTERACTIVE EXERCISES

1.   Freecycle Your Stuff

Identify three items in your home that you no longer need but could be useful to someone else. Use a local app like OfferUp, Facebook Marketplace, or Freecycle to pass them along.

2. Create a Repurposing Project

Find one item you were planning to discard and think of a creative way to give it a new life. Could an old jar become a planter? Could worn-out clothes become cleaning rags?

3. Host a Swap Party

Gather friends or neighbors for a "swap party," where everyone brings items they no longer need and exchanges them. It's a fun, social way to promote reuse and reduce waste.

CONCLUSION: SACRED CHOICES

 Consumption isn't just about what we take—it's about what we give back. Every choice we make carries a ripple effect, shaping not only the world we live in but the one we leave behind. The great apes model this for us: bonobos share food freely, orangutans use resources sparingly, and gorillas repurpose objects for play and enrichment. They remind us that survival isn't about hoarding—it's about balance, about knowing when to take, when to give, and when to let go.

In *Braiding Sweetgrass*, Robin Wall Kimmerer writes:

"Our toddlers speak of plants and animals as if they were people, extending to them self and intention and compassion—until we teach them not to."

Imagine if, instead of teaching disconnection, we nurtured that innate understanding. What if we honored objects not as disposable, but as part of a greater cycle of use and renewal? What if we saw our resources not as things to be owned but as sacred gifts, meant to be shared, repurposed, and respected?

Just as the great apes pass down skills through generations—teaching the young how to crack nuts, weave nests, and forage with care—we too must model sustainable living. We can lead by example, making the best choices we can, while ensuring that the next generation does even better.

By embracing conscious consumption, we honor the sacredness of the things we use. We give them stories, lifetimes, and meaning. And in doing so, we create a world where nothing is wasted—not objects, not opportunities, and certainly not our capacity to do better.

Chapter 10:

Beating Your Chest for Justice

"

Fight for the things that you care about, but do it in a way that will lead others to join you."

- Ruth Bader Ginsburg

SUBVERSIVE ACT

Speak up boldly for equity and compassion, using your voice, energy, and actions to advocate for change while staying grounded in resilience.

INTRODUCTION: A PRIMAL CALL FOR JUSTICE

 Justice has always required boldness. It requires us to step forward, speak out, and beat our chests for what is right. In earlier chapters, we explored how to unlearn societal "jungle rules" that hold us captive, but this chapter takes us one step further. It's not enough to dismantle the unjust norms—we must actively create new, equitable systems by advocating for others.

Injustice thrives in silence. As the haunting words from Martin Niemöller's famous post-WWII poem remind us:

"First they came for the socialists, and I did not speak out—because I was not a socialist.

Then they came for the trade unionists, and I did not speak out—because I was not a trade unionist.

Then they came for the Jews, and I did not speak out—because I was not a Jew.

Then they came for me—and there was no one left to speak for me."

History warns us that silence is complicity. Yet justice isn't just a human ideal—it's woven into the fabric of nature. Even in primate societies, justice plays a role in maintaining balance and fairness. Bonobos and chimpanzees, for example, intervene when younger or weaker individuals are bullied, showing an innate sense of fairness. It's this primal drive for equity that we must nurture within ourselves.

This chapter is a call to action: to beat our chests for justice, not out of anger or aggression but out of love and solidarity. The arc of the moral universe may be long, as Martin Luther King Jr. said, but it bends toward justice—and we are the ones who must do the bending.

PRIMATE CONNECTION: TROOP MENTALITY IN ACTION

 Primates show us that justice isn't an abstract concept—it's an instinctual behavior that fosters group harmony and survival.

✓ Bonobos: Peacemakers of the Primate World

Bonobos have been observed intervening in disputes, often siding with weaker individuals to prevent harm. Their sense of fairness helps maintain social cohesion and prevents the strong from exploiting the vulnerable (de Waal, 1997).

✓ Chimpanzees: Challenging Hierarchies

In chimpanzee troops, lower-ranking individuals sometimes form coalitions to challenge an oppressive alpha. This collaborative resistance redistributes power and ensures no single individual dominates the group (Boesch, 2001).

✓ **Gorillas: Protective Leaders**

Silverback gorillas protect their troops fiercely, stepping in to defend weaker members from predators or external threats. Their leadership prioritizes the well-being of the group over individual gain (Fossey, 1983).

These behaviors remind us that justice and advocacy aren't just intellectual ideals—they're rooted in our evolutionary history. Like our primate cousins, we can use our voices and actions to protect and uplift one another.

A HUMAN STORY: SHUTTING DOWN THE BANKS

 During the housing crisis, I joined a grassroots movement to hold banks accountable for predatory lending practices. We gathered in solidarity outside local branches, shutting them down with peaceful but unrelenting protests. It wasn't just about making noise—it was about creating real change.

I remember speaking with a family on the verge of losing their home. They looked exhausted and defeated, as though they had already accepted the loss. But when we stepped in—offering legal support, organizing community rallies, and shining a spotlight on the injustice—they began to hope again. That family, and many others, managed to keep their homes.

This reminds me of the starfish story. A person walks along the beach and sees thousands of starfish washed ashore. They begin tossing them back into the ocean one by one. When someone asks why they bother, since they can't possibly save them all, the person replies, "It made a difference to that one."

Advocating for justice can feel overwhelming. The problems are massive, systemic, and deeply entrenched. But every small act—every starfish saved—matters.

DARK THOUGHT EXPERIMENT

 Imagine a society where injustice is the norm, where people turn a blind eye to the suffering of others because they believe their voices won't make a difference. In this world, the powerful prey on the weak, knowing there's no one to hold them accountable. Human rights are stripped away incrementally, each loss met with silence until there's no one left to fight.

Now imagine the opposite: a world where every voice counts. Where people speak up not only for themselves but for those who cannot. In this world, communities come together to challenge oppression, protect the vulnerable, and build systems rooted in equity and compassion.

Which world do you want to live in? And what are you willing to do to create it?

THE NEUROSCIENCE OF ADVOCACY

Taking action for justice isn't just good for the world—it's good for your brain. When you engage in meaningful activism:

1. **Dopamine Release:** Acts of advocacy trigger the brain's reward system, releasing dopamine and creating a sense of purpose and satisfaction.

2. **Reduced Stress:** Studies show that collective action can mitigate feelings of helplessness, reducing stress and improving mental health (Klar & Kasser, 2009).

3. **Social Bonding:** Advocacy fosters connection and trust, strengthening social bonds and combatting loneliness.

Psychologically, action is the antidote to despair. By taking even small steps toward justice, we reclaim our agency and reaffirm our humanity.

INTERACTIVE EXERCISES

1. Find Your Cause

Reflect on an issue you're passionate about—whether it's racial justice, LGBTQ+ rights, environmental protection, or something else. Research organizations working on this issue and commit to one small action, such as donating, volunteering, or sharing their message.

2. Micro-Advocacy

Advocacy doesn't always mean protests or petitions. Practice "micro-advocacy" by speaking up in everyday situations. Challenge a harmful comment, support a coworker facing discrimination, or amplify a marginalized voice on social media.

3. Justice Journal

Keep a journal of your advocacy efforts. Write about the actions you've taken, the challenges you've faced, and the impact you've seen. Use this as a tool to stay motivated and reflect on your growth.

REFLECTION QUESTIONS

1. How does injustice in the world affect your mental and emotional well-being?

2. What small actions can you take to make a difference in your community?

3. How can you balance advocacy with rest and self-care to sustain your efforts over time?

CONCLUSION: BEATING THE DRUM OF JUSTICE

Justice isn't achieved overnight. It's the result of countless small acts, repeated over time, by those who refuse to surrender to fear. We are living in a dark and dangerous time—where truth is under siege, government agencies like ICE have been weaponized against the most vulnerable, and the very idea of justice is taking a beating. It is painful to witness. It is exhausting to resist. As one of the kind humans who reviewed this manuscript so wisely stated: "Action is the antidote to despair."

But remember this: even in the wild, not every ape beats their chest the loudest. Some play, some groom, some hold space for the weary. Every role in the fight for justice matters. From the bonobo diffusing conflict with connection to the orangutan outlasting the storm in quiet resilience, survival isn't just about force—it's about endurance, adaptability, and solidarity.

Injustice thrives in isolation, but a true, interconnected community has the power to dismantle it. As Martin Luther King Jr. reminded us, "The arc of the moral universe is long, but it bends toward justice." But let's be clear: it doesn't bend on its own. It bends because we bend it. Because we rise, rest, and rise again.

You don't have to break yourself to break the system. Rest when you need to. Roar when you can. And when you can't roar, drum. Let the sound of your presence—however big, however small—ripple outward. Justice doesn't just belong to the loudest voices. It belongs to all of us.

Chapter 11:

Loving Your Own Fur First

"

> "Love takes off the masks that we fear we cannot live
> without and know we cannot live within. I use the word
> "love" here not merely in the personal sense but as a
> state of being, or a state of grace - not in the infantile
> American sense of being made happy but in the tough
> and universal sense of quest and daring and growth."
>
> **- James Baldwin, The Fire Next Time**

SUBVERSIVE ACT

Cultivate self-love and self-acceptance as a radical act of defiance in a world that profits from self-doubt.

INTRODUCTION:

 This chapter is meant to complement some of the ideas explored in Chapter 4: Sacred Grooming—because, much like our primate kin, we learn best through repetition. If, by now, through reading along or the occasional glance in the mirror, you're noticing overlapping themes, then you're right where I hoped you'd be. Vines intertwine, concepts resurface, and patterns emerge—because that's how we apes learn.

Humans are not the only species that grapple with their physical forms. In the world of primates, grooming is an act of connection and care. Apes groom not only for hygiene but also to build bonds and reaffirm relationships within their communities. This simple yet profound act is their way of saying, "You are seen. You belong."

For humans, the practice of loving our own fur—our physical selves—is often more complicated. We are born into cultures that elevate unattainable ideals and train us to see our bodies as projects to fix, rather than homes to cherish. Hollywood plays a significant role in shaping these ideals, promoting archetypes of beauty that are unattainable for most. Films like *The Substance*

(2024) directed by Coralie Fargeat reflect how societal obsessions with perfection can spiral into unhealthy and unrealistic expectations, creating an environment where we are conditioned to critique rather than celebrate ourselves.

The Dalai Lama once shared a story about his shock upon learning the English term "self-hate." It was incomprehensible to him that people could hold such a harsh view of themselves. This insight speaks to a larger cultural divide and highlights the deep roots of societal conditioning that lead us away from self-acceptance. Cultivating what Buddhist psychology calls a "witness mind" can help us navigate these challenges. By observing our thoughts and experiences without attachment or judgment, we can begin to dismantle the harmful narratives we've internalized and create space for a more compassionate relationship with ourselves.

PRIMATE CONNECTION

In primate communities, grooming rituals go beyond mere cleanliness. They serve as a foundation for social cohesion, reducing stress and building trust. This tactile affirmation is a way of saying, "You matter."

✓ **Chimpanzee Self-Grooming:** Chimpanzees have been observed using tools like sticks to groom themselves, meticulously removing dirt and parasites. This act of self-care not only keeps them healthy but also reflects an innate sense of dignity.

✓ **Bonobos and Self-Soothing:** Bonobos, known for their gentle nature, engage in behaviors like hugging and self-grooming to manage stress and build a sense of comfort within themselves and their groups.

✓ **Orangutans and Mirrors:** Beyond recognizing themselves in mirrors, orangutans have been observed using mirrors to inspect and groom parts of their bodies they can't normally see, such as their faces and teeth. This behavior suggests not only self-awareness but also a desire for cleanliness and self-care.

These behaviors remind us that loving and caring for oneself is not vanity; it is a natural and necessary part of life. By observing these examples, we can learn to approach our own self-care with the same simplicity and authenticity.

HUMAN STORY

Since 2005, I have been teaching naked yoga to men, creating a brave and safe non-sexualized space for them to explore their bodies, confront their inner critics, and face what aging does to the human form. This practice is an opportunity to strip away not only clothing but also the layers of shame and judgment that society wraps around us.

Yet even in this work, I've encountered societal limitations. I have yet to create a truly inclusive space for all genders and all bodies. This reflects where we are as a culture—still hesitant, still burdened by fears and biases. While there are some welcoming spaces, like certain hot springs, even these often impose clothing requirements, signaling an enduring discomfort with vulnerability.

In my classes, I often remind participants, "I have yet to meet anyone who was born into a body they are attracted to." This truth highlights the cultural conditioning that teaches us to critique rather than celebrate ourselves. Naked yoga challenges these narratives, offering participants the chance to inhabit their bodies fully and lovingly.

DARK THOUGHT EXPERIMENT

Imagine a world where every reflective surface—every mirror, window, or screen—disappeared for a year. How would you come to know and value your body without external validation? What would change in how you see yourself and others?

Now, counter this with a second thought experiment: Imagine that every time you saw yourself reflected—on Zoom, in a mirror, or through someone else's eyes—you took a nano-moment to remind yourself: "It's wonderful to look uniquely like myself." What would this simple act of healthy narcissism—or self-affirmation—change about your relationship with your body?

INTERACTIVE EXERCISES

1. Self-Grooming Practice:

Take five minutes daily to care for your body—whether it's applying lotion, brushing your hair, or massaging your hands. Treat this as an act of love and gratitude for your physical self.

2. Mutual Massage:

Touch is a powerful act of care, yet asking for it can feel vulnerable, and receiving it isn't always easy. This exercise invites you to share a simple hand, foot, or neck massage with someone you trust—practicing both giving and receiving with awareness. Even brief, consensual touch lowers stress hormones and increases oxytocin, deepening connection and relaxation. Try it. Ask. Offer. Breathe. You are worthy of care.

3. Witness Mind Practice:

The next time you notice a critical thought about your body, pause and silently say, "I see you." Acknowledge the thought without judgment, and then replace it with a neutral or positive observation about your body.

4. Community Connection:

Organize a small gathering to discuss body positivity and self-acceptance. Share stories and encourage one another to embrace vulnerability.

EVIDENCE-BASED PRACTICES

- Research shows that mindfulness practices, such as body scans, can help individuals develop a deeper connection with and acceptance of their bodies.

- Studies on self-compassion indicate that learning to speak kindly to oneself improves body image and overall well-being.

- A 2023 survey found that 80% of people who practiced affirmations in front of a mirror for two weeks reported a significant improvement in their self-perception.

- Engaging in non-judgmental physical activities, like yoga, has been shown to reduce body dissatisfaction.

REFLECTION QUESTIONS

1. What stories have you internalized about your body, and how have they shaped your self-image?

2. How can you challenge the cultural norms that equate youth with beauty?

3. What small, subversive acts can you commit to today to reclaim love for your own fur?

4. How might you cultivate a habit of healthy narcissism or self-affirmation in your daily life?

5. How can developing a witness mind shift your relationship with your body and self-image?

SUBVERSIVE NIGHT LIVE: MIRROR WORK

Before we wrap up this chapter, let's try one more important thing. In a world that profits from your self-doubt, loving yourself is an act of rebellion—and I know that can feel like a tall order. It's not always easy to stare back at the person in the mirror when the world has spent so much time telling you you're not enough. But that's exactly why it matters.

So let's start with a little humor. Welcome to Subversive Night Live, where tonight's special guest is... you. And your first sketch? A throwback pep talk, courtesy of *Saturday Night Live's Stuart Smalley.*

A short PSA before we continue: While Al Franken's personal controversies are well-known, his SNL character offers valuable insights. Yet, many power-grabbing baboons (sorry for using baboons in vain again!), who blatantly fling monkey poo at the law while intensifying their oppressive actions without a hint of self-reflection. One wonders if these seemingly soulless humans will ever muster the courage to confront their own reflections.

Now, back to OUR monkey business. I know it might feel a little awkward to channel your inner Stuart, but awkward is often where the magic happens. So, take a deep breath, stand tall, and say it like you mean it:

"I'm good enough, I'm smart enough, and doggone it, people like me!"

And if you feel ridiculous, that's okay too. The world has conditioned us to think self-love should be easy, but sometimes the best way to approach it is to let yourself laugh through the discomfort. It's not about perfection. It's about presence. About looking yourself in the eye, without judgment, and saying:

- "I've made it through every challenge so far, and I'll make it through the next."
- "I'm allowed to rest and still be worthy of love."
- "I'm here. And I matter."
- "My happiness doesn't require permission."

And you know what? Even if it feels forced at first, it's okay. You're not trying to fool yourself; you're just breaking through the noise that tells you you're not enough. Each time you look in the mirror with compassion—even if it's a bit cheesy—you're reminding yourself that you're human, and that's the most radical thing you can be.

So laugh if you need to. Because that awkward, uncomfortable smile in the mirror? That's you, saying 'I see you, and I'm proud of you'—and there's no one else on earth who can say that like you can.

CONCLUSION: FROM ME TO WE

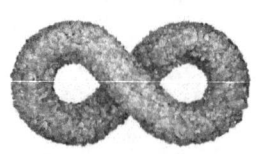

As Edward Everett Hale wrote, "I am only one, but I am one. I cannot do everything, but I can do something. And because I cannot do everything, I will not refuse to do the something that I can do."

Loving your own fur—your body, your unique expression of life—is a radical act in a world that profits from our insecurities. Start small. Start with yourself. Embrace the lessons of our primate cousins and remember that your body, as it is, is a testament to the life you've lived. By combining self-affirmation, witness mind, and community, you create ripples of self-acceptance and kindness that extend far beyond yourself.

As Brené Brown reminds us, "Owning our story and loving ourselves through that process is the bravest thing that we will ever do." It is through the process of self-acceptance and radical love that we can dismantle the harmful systems that have colonized our inner sanctuaries. Every time you choose to affirm your worth, you are engaging in an act of quiet rebellion. Every moment of self-kindness is a seed planted in the garden of collective healing.

We are not meant to fit into molds designed by others. We are meant to thrive as the unique and unrepeatable beings we are. So take this moment to honor your body, your mind, and your journey. In doing so, you not only reclaim your inner sanctuary—you help pave the way for others to do the same. Let this chapter serve as a reminder that loving yourself is not just important—it is essential for the evolution of humanity itself.

Chapter 12:

Ape-reciating All Pronouns: Evolving Language as a Tool for Healing, Not Harm

"

> "When we are in contact with our feelings and needs, we humans no longer make good slaves and underlings."
> - Marshall B. Rosenberg, Nonviolent Communication: A Language of Life

SUBVERSIVE ACT

Harness the tool of language as a force for connection, justice, and transformation. Reject the "I-It" and "Us-Them" mindset, and cultivate an "I-Thou" way of engaging with the world. Challenge the violent, divisive, and dehumanizing language that keeps us locked in cycles of separation, and instead, use words as bridges toward deeper understanding, collective healing, and social evolution.

INTRODUCTION: LANGUAGE AS A TOOL FOR LIBERATION

 Language is one of the most powerful tools we possess. It shapes our reality, influences our perceptions, and determines how we interact with the world. Words are not passive—they are weapons, medicine, maps, and cages. They can create worlds or destroy them. And for too long, we have been using them to dehumanize, to dominate, to reinforce hierarchies of oppression.

The way we speak about others—and to ourselves—determines whether we see the world through a lens of domination or a lens of connection. Philosopher Martin Buber's concept of "I-Thou" versus "I-It" relationships offers us a way to understand this. In an "I-It" framework, we treat people and the world as objects, as means to an end. This is the language of colonialism, capitalism, and oppression—where people become statistics, labels, or obstacles rather than fully realized beings. But in an "I-Thou" relationship, we recognize the full humanity of the other. We engage with reverence, curiosity, and care. We see others not as objects but as part of a shared, sacred existence.

This chapter is about reclaiming language as a tool for liberation—both personal and collective. If we are to evolve into Homo cordis et animus, we must rewrite the scripts we have been given. We must dismantle the narratives of control and replace them with ones of reciprocity and respect. We must speak the world into being—not as it is, but as it could be.

PRIMATE CONNECTION: HOW APES COMMUNICATE WITH MEANING4

The great apes, our closest evolutionary relatives, rely on sophisticated communication systems to build alliances, avoid conflict, and ensure survival. Unlike human speech, their communication is deeply embodied—it is woven into gestures, facial expressions, vocalizations, and even shared experiences of grief and play.

- ✓ **Chimpanzees:** Known for their sharp political instincts, chimps use vocal signals and body language to navigate power struggles and form social bonds. Their communication is highly intentional, with different calls signaling alarm, playfulness, and even deception.

- ✓ **Bonobos:** Unlike their aggressive chimpanzee cousins, bonobos rely on touch, vocal reassurance, and cooperative gestures to maintain peace. Their "language" is one of de-escalation and connection.

✓ **Gorillas:** Gorillas communicate primarily through deep rumbles, gestures, and eye contact. Studies have shown that individual gorillas develop unique vocalizations and signals to strengthen bonds within their troops.

✓ **Orangutans:** Often living in solitude, orangutans develop individualized ways of communicating across long distances—using deep calls that can travel through the forest for miles.

Across all great ape species, **communication is not just about conveying information**—it is about maintaining relationships, building trust, and resolving conflict. Their survival depends on it, just as ours does.

So what happens when humans forget this? When we weaponize language instead of using it to connect?

THE COST OF VIOLENT LANGUAGE AND DIVISIVE SPEECH

We are living in an era where language is increasingly being used as a tool of division. Hate speech, political propaganda, and the rise of dehumanizing rhetoric are not just moral failures—they have tangible, violent consequences.

The Impact of Language on the Brain

Neuroscience tells us that **language directly shapes our perception of reality.** Studies show that when people are repeatedly exposed to dehumanizing language (e.g., referring to immigrants as "illegals" or calling marginalized groups "animals"), their brains literally process these individuals as less human. This makes it easier to justify policies and actions that harm them.

- A study from Stanford University (2017) found that repeated exposure to dehumanizing language weakens the brain's natural empathetic response.

- Research on hate speech (Bruneau & Kteily, 2018) shows that rhetoric describing people as "vermin" or "invaders" correlates with increased support for violence against them.

- Nonviolent Communication (Rosenberg, 2003) suggests that our cultural conditioning rewards aggressive speech and punishes vulnerability, making authentic connection harder.

When we reduce people to labels—when we speak about them as "problems" rather than Thou—we lay the groundwork for apathy, exclusion, and even genocide.

But the opposite is also true: when we change our language, we change our thinking. And when we change our thinking, we change the world.

A HUMAN STORY:SPEAKING A NEW WORLD INTO BEING

I once traveled to Malaysia to see orangutans in their disappearing rainforest habitat. I stood, watching a mother and her child, and I overheard a tourist behind me say, "They look so human." Another person muttered, "No, they just act like us."

That moment struck me—how language itself reflected a hierarchy. Why do we say animals act "like us" rather than acknowledging that we, too, are animals? Why do we set ourselves apart with words instead of recognizing our shared existence?

Later, in Uganda, I observed mountain gorillas and chimpanzees—species that, despite past assumptions, were documented forming lifelong friendships. The old narratives about their "natural aggression" were wrong. New research was rewriting their story. And I wondered: How many of our own human divisions exist simply because we were told they were true?

That is the power of language. To name something is to claim it. To rewrite the words is to rewrite the world.

DARK THOUGHT EXPERIMENT: WHAT IF WE LOST OUR LANGUAGE?

Imagine a world where words are stripped of meaning—where everything is transactional, calculated, and devoid of depth. In this world, relationships are reduced to efficiency, emotions are seen as weaknesses, and people are valued only for their productivity.

Without the ability to express love, sorrow, or awe, what would life be? What would happen to art, poetry, music? What happens when the language of connection is replaced with the language of control?

Now imagine the opposite: a world where every word is chosen with care, where language is used to build, not break. What would change in how you speak? How you listen? How you think?

INTERACTIVE EXERCISES

1.   Practice "I-Thou" Language: Throughout the next week, notice how you speak to and about others. Do you treat people as full, complex beings, or as obstacles and roles? Challenge yourself to shift toward seeing and naming their full humanity.

2. Reframe Your Internal Dialogue:

The way we speak to ourselves matters. Rewrite negative self-talk in a way that affirms your worth. Instead of "I'm failing," try, "I am learning."

3. Nonviolent Communication Challenge:

For one day, practice using language that prioritizes connection over competition. Avoid blame, reframe judgment as curiosity, and express needs without aggression.

MIRROR EXERCISE: SHIFTING FROM "I-IT" TO "I-THOU"

Before diving into this practice, take a moment to ground yourself. Stand or sit comfortably in front of a mirror. Feel your body rest on the earth, let your breath slow, and remind yourself: You are safe. You are here. You are enough.

Step One: The "I-It" Experience

Now, shift your focus to your reflection. Let yourself glare, scowl, or project whatever disdain, frustration, or judgment may surface. Point directly at the mirror and, with force, declare:

"I... IT!"

Repeat it five times. Feel what arises. Notice the sensations in your body. Is there tension? Tightness? A sharpness in your breath? Does your face harden? Does your mind fill with criticisms or detachment?

After the fifth time, pause. Close your eyes. Take a slow inhale and exhale. Shake off the experience if you need to. Reground. Recenter. Return to yourself.

Step Two: The "I-Thou" Experience

Now, soften your body. Let your shoulders drop. Take a breath that feels nourishing. Look into the mirror with gentleness. See not just a reflection, but a being—a presence, a life.

Place a hand on your heart and, with warmth, say:

"I."

Then, with an open palm, gesture toward your reflection and say:

"Thou."

Repeat it five times. Let it be an offering. Notice what shifts. Does your face soften? Do your shoulders relax? How does your breath move? Do you feel more connection, more tenderness?

After the fifth time, close your eyes. Ask yourself:

- Which experience did I prefer?
- What did I feel in my body?
- What thoughts arose?
- What might this practice reveal about how I see myself?

Beyond the Mirror: Applying "I-Thou"

This exercise is not just about how you see yourself. It is about how you engage with the world.

Consider how often we default to an "I-It" mentality in our daily lives:

- The stranger in traffic becomes an obstacle.
- The customer service worker is reduced to a function.
- Animals, plants, and even objects are seen only as resources, stripped of essence.

But what happens when we shift to "I-Thou"?

- What if, instead of rushing past the cashier, we made eye contact and truly acknowledged them?

- What if we spoke to our houseplants, our pets, even our favorite coffee mug, as if they had significance?
- What if we honored the presence of a tree not as "wood to be used," but as a living being with whom we share space?

Martin Buber, who first articulated the "I-Thou" philosophy, described it as a way of relating that acknowledges the aliveness of the other—whether that "other" is a person, an animal, or the Earth itself. It is a call to presence, reverence, and reciprocity.

The way we speak to ourselves in the mirror is often the way we speak to the world. And the way we treat the world is a reflection of how we treat ourselves.

So, as you close this practice, consider:

- Where in your life do you default to "I-It"?
- How might you bring more "I-Thou" into your relationships—with people, nature, and even the objects around you?
- What small, subversive acts of reverence could you bring into your daily life?

The revolution begins in the mirror. Let it ripple outward.

CONCLUSION: WORDS AS BLUEPRINTS FOR EVOLUTION

 If we are to evolve, we must first change the way we speak—to

ourselves, to each other, and to the world. Our words are blueprints for the future we want to build. The old narratives of domination, division, and disposability have brought us to the brink. It is time to write new ones.

As mentioned earlier in the book, Thich Nhat Hanh teaches in his philosophy of Interbeing, nothing exists in isolation. Everything is connected, and our words—like seeds—have the power to grow either destruction or compassion.

The question now is simple: What story will you choose to tell and dare you be the Hero of that tale?

Chapter 13

Swinging Offline: Digital Detox for Primal Clarity

"

> "*Almost everything will work again if you unplug it for a few minutes, including you.*"
>
> **- Anne Lamott**

SUBVERSIVE ACT

Reclaim Your Attention: Unplugging from digital distractions is an act of radical self-care and rebellion in a world designed to keep you tethered. By intentionally disconnecting, you reclaim your focus, foster clarity, and reconnect with the natural rhythms of life.

INTRODUCTION

 Imagine the freedom of a day with no notifications, no emails, and no endless scrolling. Our ancestors thrived without digital distractions, relying on their senses, instincts, and the natural rhythms of the earth. Today, the digital world colonizes our attention, demanding more of our energy than ever before. While technology has its place, our overdependence on it disconnects us from the very essence of being human.

This chapter invites you to unplug and experience the primal clarity that comes with living offline. Studies show that digital detoxes improve focus, reduce anxiety, and deepen our connection to ourselves and the world around us. When you step away from the screen, you open the door to the richness of real life.

MY STORY: FAILING TO UNPLUG

I wish I could say that I've mastered the art of digital detoxing, but the truth is, I've failed more times than I can count. I've deleted apps, only to reinstall them days later. I've tried "no phone Sundays" and ended up sneaking a glance at my email before noon. The lure of social media, with its endless updates and dopamine hits, is powerful—and I'm not alone in this struggle.

What finally gave me hope wasn't another app promising to track my screen time, but rather an unlikely source: gorillas. Gorillas in captivity have been observed using tools intentionally, such as sticks to retrieve food or branches for support. Interestingly, these same gorillas rarely use tools in the wild. Researchers suggest that in captivity, where their natural rhythms are disrupted, gorillas adapt by using tools more frequently and deliberately. This insight hit home for me: could I, too, learn to use technology intentionally rather than habitually?

The answer lay in adopting a mindset similar to these gorillas. Instead of letting technology control me, I began to ask: "What is the purpose of this tool, and how does it serve my well-being?" By shifting my perspective, I started using technology with greater intention, treating it as a resource rather than a reflex.

LEARNING FROM THE AMISH

Another source of inspiration came from the Amish community. Known for their selective use of technology, the Amish don't reject modern tools outright. Instead, they introduce new technologies on a trial basis, carefully observing their impact on the community. If a tool enhances their values of simplicity, connection, and sustainability, it stays. If it disrupts those values, it's set aside.

What if we adopted a similar approach? Imagine testing a new app or device with questions like:

- Does this improve my life or complicate it?
- Does it help me connect with others in meaningful ways?
- Does it align with my values?

By treating technology as something to be evaluated rather than automatically accepted, we can reclaim control over our digital lives.

CONTEMPLATING AI INTEGRATION

The irony isn't lost on me: here I am, writing a book about digital detox while relying on AI—an extraordinary tool—to help me get the words down. Without AI, I might never have had the courage to write this book. But what does this mean for balance? Does AI free me to spend more time gardening, meditating, and connecting with nature? Or does it entice me to write more books, pulling me deeper into the digital realm? Time will tell. For now, I'm with you, struggling to find harmony between the benefits and the temptations of technology.

AI can be a double-edged sword. Used wisely, it can amplify our creativity and productivity. Misused, it risks tethering us even more tightly to our screens. The key lies in intentionality: viewing tools like AI as collaborators rather than masters, ensuring they serve our well-being rather than the other way around.

And, there's a deeper risk—one that extends beyond personal use. AI is shaped by those who program it, and in the wrong hands, it can become a tool of manipulation rather than liberation. For instance, in working on this last edition of my imperfect offering to the world, ChatGPT has already shifted how it responds to my exploration of current politics. Governments, corporations, and powerful entities can use AI to control narratives, exploit biases, and reinforce existing power structures. If we aren't vigilant, the very tools designed to enhance knowledge and connection could instead be wielded to limit free thought and amplify misinformation. The question isn't just how we use AI— it's how we ensure it remains a force for empowerment rather than control.

STORIES OF HARMONY WITH TOOLS:

1. Shinrin-Yoku (Forest Bathing) Meets Technology: A small community in Japan integrates mindfulness apps with their practice of forest bathing. The app gently guides participants to focus on sensory details—the sound of rustling leaves, the smell of the forest floor—then prompts them to log their reflections offline. This hybrid approach enhances the experience without disrupting it.

2. Farmers and Precision Agriculture: In parts of Africa, farmers use simple apps to track weather patterns and optimize planting schedules. These tools, used sparingly and purposefully,

help increase crop yields without overwhelming traditional practices.

3. Artists and Digital Tools: Many visual artists today blend traditional techniques with digital platforms. For instance, a painter might sketch by hand, then refine their work digitally, merging old and new to create something uniquely modern yet timeless.

These examples remind us that technology can complement, not compete with, our humanity when used with care and intentionality.

INTERACTIVE EXERCISES

1. Sunrise Reset:

Watch a sunrise or sunset without a phone. Focus on the colors, sounds, and sensations.

2. Digital Sabbath:

Dedicate one day a week to being offline. Use this time to journal, connect with loved ones, or enjoy nature.

3. Silent Walks:

Take a walk in nature without music or podcasts. Let the sounds of the earth guide you back to your primal self.

4. Tool Trial:

Select one app or device you use regularly and evaluate its impact. Keep a journal of how it influences your mood, focus, and well-being.

5. AI Reflection:

Reflect on how you use AI or digital tools. Write down one way it has helped you grow and one way it might hold you back.

COGNITIVE LIBERTY AND RECLAIMING YOUR INNER SANCTUARY

At the core of human freedom lies cognitive liberty— the right to control our own minds, to think, dream, and perceive without external coercion. In an age where algorithms predict our desires before we even name them, where governments dictate what substances we may or may not ingest, and where social conditioning shapes our beliefs before we fully awaken to them, cognitive liberty is not just a philosophical ideal—it is an act of defiance.

Philosophers from John Stuart Mill to Aldous Huxley have warned us about the dangers of external forces manipulating thought. Mill's *On Liberty* argued that true freedom demands sovereignty over our own consciousness, while Huxley foresaw a world where control wouldn't come through force, but through the dulling of the mind—where people, distracted and pacified, would willingly surrender their autonomy. Today, we see this struggle play out in battles over access to psychedelics, the fight against mass surveillance, and the quiet war waged against critical thinking itself.

And then there's the media machine, feeding us a steady diet of outrage, distraction, and algorithmically optimized noise. The more we consume, the more our cognitive bandwidth gets clogged, making it harder to think for ourselves, to sit in stillness, to hear our own inner voice. This isn't a side note—it's central to the conversation. Reclaiming our inner sanctuary means taking back our attention, not just from those who wish to control us, but from the systems designed to keep us too distracted to even notice.

And let's be real—if we were still swinging from the trees, we wouldn't be doom-scrolling TikTok until our brains melted. Other primates spend their days grooming each other, bonding, and foraging with focus. We? We've outsourced our grooming to influencers, our foraging to the algorithm, and our social cohesion to whatever keeps us the most outraged.

But there's another way—a return to primal clarity. When a chimp locks eyes with you, there's no filter, no distortion—just raw presence. Orangutans don't waste time overanalyzing their place in the hierarchy of Instagram. Bonobos don't lose sleep doom-spiraling over political clickbait. Their clarity isn't just instinct—it's survival. And maybe, just maybe, reclaiming our own cognitive freedom means stripping away the noise and remembering how to be fully, unapologetically present.

This topic deserves far more attention than a few paragraphs can hold. I admit, this is far from an afterthought—it's an invitation. Because if we don't guard our minds, someone else will. And the ones waiting to do so aren't exactly looking out for our best interests.

So instead of scrolling online, maybe as you set down this book, lock eyes with that beautiful ape in the mirror, and see if who stares back at you is ready for some primal clarity.

CONCLUSION: A MIND IS A TERRIBLE THING TO CAGE

 Unplugging is not about rejecting technology but about reclaiming your attention and energy. As the Amish teach us, technology can be a tool for good when used intentionally. As gorillas show us, deliberate adaptation can transform disruption into opportunity. As AI reminds us, tools can inspire creativity without defining us.

In the words of Wendell Berry, "To cherish what remains of the Earth and to foster its renewal is our only legitimate hope of survival." Disconnecting allows us to reconnect with the deeper rhythms of life—the call of nature, the joy of play, and the clarity of stillness.

In a world dominated by screens, stepping offline is a subversive act of self-care and rebellion. Take the leap, and rediscover the richness of life lived fully present. By doing so, you become part of a larger movement toward harmony, balance, and intentional living—a movement that honors the best of what it means to be human.

Chapter 14:

Reclaiming the Commons: Shared Spaces, Shared Futures

"

"True peace is not merely the absence of tension; it is the presence of justice."

- Martin Luther King Jr.

SUBVERSIVE ACT

Challenge the privatization and neglect of communal spaces. Reclaim the commons as places of connection, belonging, and collective care.

INTRODUCTION: THE COMMONS LOST AND FOUND

 *"What is Urinetown?"* they ask in the satirical musical of the same name. The answer? A world where even **peeing** is privatized. Ridiculous? Maybe. But not so far from the creeping reality we face today.

First staged in 2001 and directed by John Rando, *Urinetown: The Musical* satirizes a world where private corporations control the most basic human needs, forcing people to pay for the right to relieve themselves. Those who can't afford it? Exiled or worse. The play was meant as an absurd dystopia, a commentary on unchecked capitalism, environmental degradation, and authoritarian control. But the joke is on us—because in many ways, we're already there.

The slow, deliberate erosion of the commons—the spaces and resources that once belonged to all of us—is well underway. Public parks fall into disrepair, libraries face relentless budget cuts, and city planning prioritizes profit over people. Once-vibrant gathering places are replaced by private developments, and even our digital commons—once a space of free expression—has become a marketplace for surveillance and misinformation. What was once shared is now controlled, priced, and restricted.

The commons have always been more than just places; they are the physical and symbolic foundation of cooperation, dialogue, and collective identity. When we lose them, we lose more than access—we lose a fundamental part of what binds us together. The erosion of these spaces isn't just an inconvenience; it's a methodical dismantling of public power, a quiet restructuring of society where isolation replaces connection, and private interests dictate the limits of our freedom.

And yet, history reminds us: the commons are never lost without a fight. From medieval peasants resisting enclosures to modern movements reclaiming urban spaces, people have always found ways to push back, to gather, to insist that some things should belong to everyone.

So, what happens when we lose these shared spaces? What happens to us? More importantly—what can we do to reclaim them?

PRIMATE CONNECTION: SHARED SPACES IN THE ANIMAL KINGDOM

 Apes and other social animals thrive in environments that encourage cooperation and mutual care. Their survival depends

on their ability to share resources, resolve conflicts, and create harmony within their groups.

✓ Chimpanzees: Resource Sharing

In the wild, chimpanzees often share food, especially when it comes to high-value resources like meat. This sharing reinforces social bonds and ensures the survival of the group. However, it's not without conflict—chimps will fight over access to resources, reminding us of the delicate balance between individual needs and collective well-being.

✓ Bonobos: Communal Cohesion

Bonobos, often called the "hippie apes," demonstrate how shared spaces can promote peace and connection. Their egalitarian social structures are maintained through mutual grooming, play, and the communal use of resources. They teach us that cooperation, rather than competition, can be a foundation for thriving communities.

✓ Elephants: Guardians of Shared Waterholes

While not apes, elephants provide a powerful example of how animals protect shared spaces. In drought-stricken regions, elephant matriarchs lead their herds to waterholes, often coordinating with other herds to ensure that everyone gets access. These shared water sources are lifelines, and their survival depends on collective stewardship.

THE RISKS WE FACE: PRIVATIZATION AND ALIENATION

The erosion of the commons has far-reaching consequences for individuals and society as a whole.

1. Loss of Connection

When public spaces are replaced by privatized ones, opportunities for connection and community diminish. Parks, libraries, and community centers are not just physical spaces—they are places where people gather, share stories, and build relationships. Without them, loneliness and isolation grow.

2. Environmental Degradation

The privatization of natural resources often leads to exploitation and destruction. Forests are clear-cut for profit, water is bottled and sold, and public lands are turned into industrial zones. This destruction doesn't just harm the environment—it harms us all.

3. Economic Inequality

The privatization of shared resources exacerbates inequality. When public services like education, healthcare, and transportation are turned into profit-driven enterprises, those who can't afford them are left behind. This creates a cycle of poverty and exclusion that is difficult to break.

A HUMAN STORY: RECLAIMING A NEIGHBORHOOD

In a small urban neighborhood, a vacant lot sat unused for years. It was overgrown with weeds, littered with trash, and avoided by residents. But one day, a group of neighbors decided to transform it. They cleared the debris, planted a community garden, and built benches and a play area.

The space became a hub of activity. Parents brought their children to play, elderly residents gathered to chat, and local artists painted murals on the surrounding walls. The garden produced fresh vegetables that were shared among the community, and the once-ignored lot became a symbol of hope and resilience.

This transformation wasn't easy. The neighbors faced pushback from developers who wanted to buy the land and turn it into a parking lot. But their collective action and determination won out. They proved that reclaiming the commons is not just about creating spaces—it's about creating possibilities.

DARK THOUGHT EXPERIMENT

Imagine a world where all public spaces are gone. Schools, parks, libraries, and even sidewalks are privatized. Without shared spaces, people retreat into their homes, isolated from one another. Community disappears, replaced by competition and alienation. What does this world feel like? How does it function?

Now imagine the opposite: a world where the commons are cherished and expanded. Every neighborhood has parks, gardens, and gathering places. Resources like water and energy are shared equitably, and people take pride in caring for their communities. In this world, connection thrives, and the well-being of one is seen as the well-being of all. Which world will you help create?

INTERACTIVE EXERCISES

1.   Reclaim a Space

Identify a neglected space in your community—a vacant lot, a rundown park, or an unused corner—and imagine how it could be transformed. Start small: organize a cleanup day, plant flowers, or gather neighbors for a brainstorming session.

2. Participate in the Digital Commons

The digital commons holds immense potential—but like any shared space, it thrives only when people actively engage. Platforms like **BlueSky** offer alternatives to corporate-controlled spaces, while **Reddit** fosters collective knowledge-sharing. Even ad-heavy platforms like Facebook and Instagram still function as imperfect public squares. Nextdoor.com, though flawed, aspires to connect real-life neighbors, and **Signal** provides an encrypted space where many create safe, private group discussions.

The question isn't just where we participate but how. The digital commons, like its physical counterpart, needs care, intention, and stewardship. What role will you play in keeping it truly open?

3. Shared Resources Challenge

For one week, commit to sharing resources with others. This could mean carpooling, sharing tools with neighbors, or participating in a community swap. Reflect on how this changes your sense of connection and community.

ANOTHER HUMAN STORY: LEARNING FROM EACH OTHER'S COMMON GROUND

Travel has a way of shifting perspectives, not by proving one place "better" than another, but by reminding us of the many ways people choose to create and sustain community. When I visited Taiwan for Taipei Pride, I was struck by how a densely packed city still prioritized public spaces for everyone. Parks weren't just green patches between buildings—they were living, breathing extensions of the community. Free outdoor gyms, playgrounds for all ages, and acupressure rock gardens invited people to slow down, take off their shoes, and connect—with nature, with their bodies, with each other.

In Mexico City, I found another small but powerful reminder of shared space. Along bustling sidewalks, comfortable benches were built into advertising booths, turning what could have been just another commercialized structure into a resting place for weary pedestrians. These are simple things, yet they speak volumes about a society's values.

I'm not here to say that "over there" is good and "here" is bad. What I am saying is that it's refreshing—and necessary—to see places that, against all odds, are expanding public spaces rather than shuttering them. In a world that often prioritizes profit over people, these small acts of common ground feel like radical invitations to slow down, sit down, and belong. By learning from how others prioritize public space, we can rethink how we design our own communities—not to compete, but to connect.

CONCLUSION: A BRAVE AND SHARED FUTURE

 Reclaiming the commons is not just an act of resistance—it's an act of hope. It's a declaration that we belong to each other, that our fates are intertwined, and that our shared spaces and resources are worth fighting for.

In his teachings on interbeing, Thich Nhat Hanh reminds us that "we are here to awaken from the illusion of our separateness." This awakening begins in the commons, where we come together to share, care, and build a future rooted in connection and compassion.

Yes, there are risks. Reclaiming the commons requires courage, persistence, and a willingness to challenge powerful systems. But the rewards are profound. When we create brave spaces—not necessarily safe ones—we open the door to growth, healing, and transformation.

Imagine a world where interdependence is celebrated, where shared spaces are abundant, and where every person has a place to belong. This is the vision of Homo cordis et animus—a species that embodies both the heart and the wild. It's a bold vision, but it's one worth striving for. So let's swing boldly into the future, reclaiming the commons and building a world that honors our shared humanity.

Where the Wild Things Mourn: Embracing the End

"

"To love and to lose is the most beautiful and terrifying thing we can do. If we refuse the grief, we also refuse the love."

- Francis Weller

SUBVERSIVE ACT

Face mortality with courage and grace. Build your grief capacity and learn practical strategies to cope with death anxiety (thanaphobia) as pathways to live more fully, love more deeply, and honor the impermanence of life.

A TENDER MOMENT BETWEEN MOTHER AND CHILD

While visiting the Bwindi Impenetrable Forest in Uganda, I had the great honor of sitting with a troop of mountain gorillas and witnessed a most touching moment between a two-year-old baby and his mother. The mother had sustained some injuries—perhaps from a scuffle with another ape. Even though they are relatively peaceful beings, they still must work out their differences.

After the baby finished nursing from his mother, who was recovering from her injuries, he looked at the wound on her upper chest and tenderly licked his fingers before lightly caressing the open wound. I wondered how much awareness our close relatives have of mortality and vulnerability. The mother cradled the caring child in her arms after he provided some instinctual first aid. The potency of his touch and the love in her arms—it would not last forever, but this mother-son bonding moment will forever remain in my heart.

Watching them, I saw not just the depth of their connection but the inevitability of loss. One day, this baby will grow into a strong silverback, and his mother will fade from his world, as all mothers do. This cycle is the unspoken truth that binds us all—gorilla and human alike. We live, we love, and one day, we must let go. Yet, in this moment, as he tended to her wound, he embodied the tenderness and care that make grief so profound.

This is the love we apes are all capable of, and the grief we share when it is over is the rent we pay for living and loving. It is not just the pain of loss, but the recognition that to have shared such love is a privilege. As we navigate our own relationships with mortality, may we remember that even in the animal kingdom, there is space for compassion, caregiving, and deep, abiding connection—proof that love and grief are woven into the very fabric of existence.

INTRODUCTION: THE DANCE OF IMPERMANENCE

 We are born into a world where loss is inevitable, yet we spend much of our lives resisting this truth. From an early age, we are shielded from death, taught to fear it, or at best, to ignore it. Our culture reinforces this avoidance with euphemisms, rushed funeral services, and an expectation to move on quickly from grief. But what if, instead of avoiding death, we leaned into it?

What if we treated mortality as a profound teacher rather than an unwelcome intruder?

Grief is the shadow side of love, an inseparable companion to the joy of connection. As Stephen Jenkinson describes, we live in a culture of death phobia—one that pathologizes grief and silences our conversations around loss. Yet, as Francis Weller reminds us, to refuse grief is to refuse love itself. When we acknowledge death rather than deny it, we cultivate a deeper presence in life. We allow ourselves to grieve, to love fiercely, and to live with greater awareness of our own impermanence.

During a psychedelic journey, my spirit guide came to me and said, "Grief will not kill you, but not grieving will harm you immensely." That truth struck me deeply. I've seen how unexpressed grief poisons the heart, leading to depression, addiction, and physical illness. As a grief therapist, I've come to understand that holding space for grief is one of the most radical acts of love. In those moments of vulnerability, I remind my clients that they can feel deeply without being consumed—and in doing so, they reclaim their humanity.

This chapter is an invitation to shift our perspective on death. Instead of treating it as an adversary, we will explore how embracing mortality can deepen our relationships, ground us in the present moment, and guide us toward a more meaningful existence. Grief is not a weakness. It is a portal to healing, a bridge between the seen and unseen, and a sacred act of remembering.

An Invitation to Shift Perspective

This chapter is an offering, a gentle invitation to see death not as an adversary but as a teacher. Each of us grapples with this in our own way—there is no right or wrong path, only the one that is yours to walk. Embracing mortality can deepen our relationships, root us in the present, and guide us toward a more meaningful existence.

Grief is not a weakness. It is a portal to healing, a bridge between the seen and unseen, a sacred act of remembering. And if any of this stirs something in you— if resistance, discomfort, or uncertainty arise—return to chapter one. Be kind to yourself. Let gentleness be your guide. This book exists to affirm you, to remind you that you are already whole, already worthy.

From one mindful mortal to another, I am just a fellow somebody here to remind EVERYONE that you are a very precious SOMEBODY. Your life counts even though it may not feel that way at times.

HELPFUL TIPS ON SWINGING ON THE VINES OF THIS CHAPTER

This chapter will guide you through an exploration of death anxiety and how grief, rather than being a burden, can be a profound tool for transformation. We will examine:

1. Thanatophobia and its impact on daily life.

2.   The cultural and psychological roots of our fear of death.

3.   Ways to cultivate a healthier relationship with mortality through practical strategies, therapy, and spiritual traditions.

4.   How grief manifests in humans and non-human primates, demonstrating its universality.

5.   Rituals and traditions from around the world that honor mourning and loss.

6.   Resources to support your journey in reframing your relationship with death.

Let us move with the rhythm of impermanence, swinging on the vines of life and death, singing the song of love, loss, and everything in between.

THANATOPHOBIA: WHEN FEAR OF DEATH BECOMES PARALYZING

For many, death is not just an abstract concept—it is an intrusive, terrifying thought. The mere mention of it can send shivers down the spine, triggering existential dread and avoidance. Thanatophobia, the persistent fear of death, manifests in countless ways: hypervigilance over health, an inability to discuss mortality, or compulsive distractions to evade confronting impermanence. While fear of death is natural, unchecked thanatophobia can stifle our ability to truly live.

Stephen Jenkinson speaks of a culture of death phobia— one that medicates, sanitizes, and distances itself from death at every turn. Thich Nhat Hanh, in contrast, reminds us that "the fear of death comes from not knowing how to live." The antidote to thanatophobia is not avoidance but engagement—a conscious willingness to explore mortality as an intrinsic part of existence rather than its negation.

ADDITIONAL CULTURAL PERSPECTIVES ON MOURNING

While many cultures suppress grief, others embrace it as a crucial part of life. Expanding on traditional mourning rituals, we can look at a few more profound global traditions:

- **Tibetan Sky Burials** – In Tibetan Buddhism, the dead are offered to vultures in an act of generosity, reinforcing the cycle of life. This practice helps communities confront death directly, without fear.

- **Día de los Muertos** (Day of the Dead, Mexico) – A vibrant and celebratory remembrance of ancestors, combining ritual offerings (ofrendas), food, and storytelling to keep the connection with the deceased alive.

- **Ghanaian Fantasy Coffins** – In Ghana, customized coffins shaped like symbolic objects (animals, cars, tools) honor the deceased's life and passions, celebrating their unique journey rather than mourning their loss alone.

These traditions teach us that grief can be shared, ritualized, and even joyful. They remind us that how we hold grief is a choice—one that can empower us to integrate loss into our lives meaningfully.

STRENGTHENING THE CALL TO ACTION

As we approach the final sections of this chapter, consider asking yourself:

- ✓ **How do I personally engage with grief?** Do I avoid it, suppress it, or honor it?

- ✓ **What rituals or conversations can I introduce into my life to normalize discussions about death?**

- ✓ **What can I learn from cultural traditions or historical practices that can help me feel more at peace with impermanence?**

- ✓ **Who in my life can I support in their grieving process, knowing that communal grief is essential to healing?**

Grief and death do not have to be isolating experiences. They can be doorways into a deeper appreciation of life and love.

THE ROOTS OF THANATOPHOBIA

- **Cultural Avoidance of Death** – Many modern societies treat death as something to be fought, hidden, or delayed indefinitely, reinforcing denial rather than acceptance.

- **Loss of Communal Rituals** – Traditional mourning practices once provided structured ways to process loss, but today, many are left to grieve in isolation.

- **Unresolved Grief and Trauma** – Past losses, especially those experienced without adequate support, can deepen anxiety about one's own mortality.

- **Fear of the Unknown** – The ambiguity surrounding what happens after death can provoke distress, especially in those who seek certainty.

- **Attachment to Identity and Ego** – The fear of 'ceasing to exist' is often tied to our sense of self and control over our lives.

BEYOND FEAR: A PATH TOWARD PEACE

1. Develop a Relationship with Mortality

- Engage in mindful contemplation of death rather than suppressing it.

- Practice memento mori, an ancient Stoic tradition of reflecting on death to foster appreciation for life.

- Spend time in cemeteries, engage in ancestral remembrance, or attend death cafés to normalize conversations about mortality.

2. Embrace Death Literacy

- Read works like Die Wise by Stephen Jenkinson and No Death, No Fear by Thich Nhat Hanh.

- **The Life of Death (YouTube Video)**

A beautifully hand-drawn short film by Marsha Onderstijn, The Life of Death portrays Death as a compassionate presence rather than a fearsome entity. This gentle and profound animation invites us to rethink our relationship with mortality. Watch it here:

https://youtu.be/ofnCdC8P70g?si=DgJO5WPx4r5wWez4

- Learn about various end-of-life practices, including green burials, home funerals, and legacy planning.
- Explore different cultural and spiritual perspectives on death and the afterlife to expand understanding and comfort.

3. **Create Personal Rituals**

- Write your own obituary or farewell letter as a reflection exercise.
- Establish a gratitude practice that acknowledges life's impermanence.
- Designate meaningful items or words to pass on to loved ones as a way of engaging with legacy and continuity.

4. **Engage in Grief and Thanatophobia Therapy**

- Work with a therapist trained in grief integration to explore unresolved losses and fears.
- Consider Holotrophic Breathwork or (when available) psychedelic-assisted

therapy to experience ego dissolution and interconnectedness, reducing death anxiety.

- Seek guidance from death doulas, spiritual caregivers, or end-of-life practitioners who specialize in navigating these conversations.

5. Foster Community Around Mortality

- Join groups that openly discuss death, such as The Order of the Good Death or Let's Reimagine.

- Participate in grief circles where mourning is communal rather than solitary.

- Advocate for healthier cultural narratives around death and dying.

PRIMATE CONNECTION: HOW APES MOURN

Our primate relatives grieve in ways that are hauntingly familiar, reminding us that grief is not uniquely human—it's a shared thread that runs through the animal kingdom. I mentioned a personal encounter with a parent-child Mountain Gorilla earlier in this chapter and there is so much more that we can learn from all of the Great Apes. Here are just a few examples:

✓ **Chimpanzees: Silent Vigils**

When a chimpanzee dies, their troop often gathers around the body in silence, touching it gently and sitting vigil. Mothers who lose infants may carry the bodies for days or weeks, showing visible signs of distress and reluctance to let go (Anderson et al., 2010). Researchers have also observed chimpanzees engaging in what appears to be grief-like behavior, returning to the site of a death repeatedly and displaying subdued emotions for days.

✓ Bonobos: Collective Consolation

Bonobos grieve as a group, comforting one another with touch and grooming. Their collective mourning strengthens social bonds and provides emotional support to those most affected by the loss. Scientists studying bonobos have found that those experiencing grief seek out and receive more social contact from others in their troop, reinforcing the idea that communal mourning is a core part of primate life.

✓ Gorillas: Emotional Resonance

Dian Fossey observed gorillas mourning the death of a silverback named Digit. The troop members sat in a circle around his body, quietly touching him and each other. Their grief was palpable, a communal acknowledgment of their loss. More recent studies have confirmed that gorillas will often stay close to deceased members, sometimes swaying and vocalizing in what seems to be a ritual of sorrow.

✓ Orangutans: Maternal Grief

Orangutan mothers, like chimpanzees, have been observed carrying the bodies of their deceased infants for days or even weeks. In some cases, they continue to groom the lifeless bodies, seemingly unable to let go. This behavior reflects a deep maternal bond and suggests an awareness of loss that extends beyond simple instinct.

✓ Japanese Macaques: Mourning in Motion

Though not technically great apes, Japanese macaques have also been observed engaging in grief-like behaviors. In documented cases, macaques have been seen carrying the bodies of deceased infants for extended periods, even adjusting their behavior to accommodate the weight of the body as it decomposes. Their mourning process mirrors patterns seen in humans, where letting go of a loved one is often gradual and filled with ritualistic actions.

These behaviors reveal that mourning is not a sign of weakness but a testament to love and connection. Grief is as natural as breathing and as essential as community. The way primates express their loss serves as a profound mirror for our own experiences—reminding us that love, loss, and the rituals of remembrance are deeply ingrained in our evolutionary history. In witnessing their grief, we are invited to embrace our own, understanding that it is not something to be feared but rather a sacred act that binds us to those we have loved and lost.

ACTIVE GRIEF: LESSONS FROM HUMAN CULTURES THAT HONOR MOURNING

While many modern societies suppress grief, others embrace it as a natural and necessary part of life.

1. Keening in Celtic Traditions

The Celts practiced keening—vocal wailing led by women at funerals. This unrestrained expression of grief allowed mourners to release their sorrow fully, creating a communal space for healing.

2. Jewish Shiva

In Jewish tradition, families observe shiva after a death, sitting in mourning for seven days. During this time, friends and neighbors visit to offer support, bringing food and companionship to ease the burden of loss.

3. African-American Funeral Traditions

For many African-American communities, funerals serve as both a solemn farewell and a vibrant celebration of life. Rooted in resilience, faith, and deep cultural traditions, these gatherings provide space for mourning, remembrance, and collective healing. Music, gospel singing, and storytelling play essential roles, offering comfort and honoring the legacy of the deceased. At times, the service may include joyful expressions—clapping, dancing, or "homegoing" celebrations—reflecting a belief in reunion beyond this life.

4. Wailing Rooms for Holocaust Survivors

After World War II, therapists working with Holocaust survivors created "wailing rooms," safe spaces where survivors could scream, cry, and release their grief. These rooms were a powerful reminder that grief must be expressed, not suppressed.

THE COST OF UNRESOLVED GRIEF

Unprocessed grief doesn't disappear—it finds other ways to manifest. Research shows that unresolved grief can have significant physical, emotional, and psychological consequences. Some of the most well-documented effects include:

- **Increased risk of heart disease and high blood pressure:** Studies have found that individuals experiencing prolonged grief have a 41% increased risk of heart-related conditions, including heart attacks and hypertension (Lannen et al., 2008).

- **Weakened immune function:** Research has shown that grief can suppress immune system responses, making individuals more vulnerable to infections and chronic illnesses (Stroebe et al., 2007).

- **Mental health struggles:** People experiencing unresolved grief are more likely to develop depression, anxiety, and substance abuse disorders. A study in JAMA Psychiatry found that prolonged grief disorder (PGD) affects nearly 10% of bereaved individuals, leading to significant impairment in daily life (Shear et al., 2011).

- **Higher mortality rates:** A Harvard Medical School study found that individuals who lose a spouse have a 66% increased risk of dying within the first three months following their partner's death, often due to a combination of stress-induced cardiovascular events and immune system decline (Elwert & Christakis, 2008).

- **Complicated grief:** Unlike ordinary grief, complicated grief is a condition where intense mourning interferes with daily life for an extended period, preventing emotional healing and increasing the risk of long-term psychological distress.

In a society that puts time limits on mourning, pathologizes prolonged grief, and avoids death altogether, these consequences are tragically common. Living in a death-avoidant culture makes it harder to grieve, but it also makes it more essential. By acknowledging grief, we allow ourselves to process it in a healthier way, reducing the risk of these long-term effects and ultimately fostering a deeper appreciation for life and love.

DARK THOUGHT EXPERIMENT

 Imagine a world where grief is silenced. No one cries, no one mourns, and loss is met with cold indifference. In this world, people carry the weight of their pain alone, disconnected from their emotions and one another. Without the rituals of

remembrance, the bonds that tie us to our ancestors, to our communities, and to our own humanity begin to fray.

Children are taught that sadness is a burden, that tears are a weakness, and that moving on is the only acceptable response to loss. Funerals are reduced to administrative tasks—brief and impersonal. Graves go untended, and memories fade as if those who once lived had never existed at all. The echoes of love, which should endure through the act of mourning, are stifled before they can take root.

Now imagine the cost of this emotional suppression. Research tells us that unresolved grief increases the risk of heart disease, weakens the immune system, and leaves people vulnerable to mental health disorders. But beyond the biological toll, what does this grief-starved world do to the soul? What happens to a culture that no longer acknowledges the depth of its losses?

Now consider the opposite: a world where grief is embraced. In this world, loss is not something to be endured in solitude but carried together, woven into the fabric of daily life. Communities gather to mourn, to wail, to remember. Love is understood as something so deep that it must be grieved when it is lost. And in this acknowledgment of sorrow, life itself becomes richer.

Which world do you want to manifest?

CONCLUSION: BEFRIENDING THE HEART OF GRIEF

 Grief is the price we pay for love, but it is also a gift. It is the proof that we have loved deeply, and that love never truly dies—it transforms. To grieve is to honor what was, to acknowledge our connection to the past, and to weave that love into the fabric of our ongoing lives.

This is not easy work. It demands that we be present with pain, that we resist the cultural urge to minimize or bypass loss, and that we hold space for the complexity of emotions that accompany death. But this is the work humans were built for. Our ancestors sat in circles, sang songs of remembrance, and carried grief together as a sacred responsibility. We are no different.

Fear of death, or thanatophobia, often stems from an unwillingness to engage with grief and impermanence. When we resist the reality of death, we also resist fully embracing life. By acknowledging our mortality, we create space for deeper appreciation, meaningful relationships, and a greater sense of purpose. In this way, confronting thanatophobia is not just about easing fear—it is about expanding our capacity to love and live with intention. It is a call to reclaim our rightful place in the continuum of existence, to see death not as a threat but as an integral part of life's rhythm.

In a time when the world often feels fragmented, grief can be a radical act of connection. It reminds us that we belong to each other, that love is never wasted, and that even in sorrow, we can find meaning. We have a moral obligation—not just to ourselves but to one another—to keep this awareness alive, to resist the numbing pull of avoidance, and to remind each other, again and again, that mourning is an act of courage.

So let us grieve deeply. Let us support one another in our sorrow. And let us, with daring and creativity, swing on the vines of life—knowing that love and loss are entwined, and that both are worth embracing.

ADDITIONAL RESOURCES

Organizations & Communities

- **INELDA (International End of Life Doula Association)**

A leading organization that trains and certifies end-of-life doulas, providing compassionate guidance for those navigating death and dying. Learn more at INELDA.

- **The Order of the Good Death**

Founded by Caitlin Doughty, this movement advocates for death positivity and helps individuals explore meaningful end-of-life practices. More at Order of the Good Death.

- **Let's Reimagine**

Visit letsreimagine.org, a platform dedicated to transforming the way we approach life, loss, and death. Through community events, workshops, and storytelling, Reimagine offers a compassionate space to explore grief, end-of-life care, and what it means to live fully.

- **What's Your Grief**

Check out whatsyourgrief.org, an online resource offering practical tools and compassionate insights for navigating loss. The site features articles, courses, and a vibrant community forum where people can share their stories and support one another through the grieving process.

ADDITIONAL THANATOPHOBIA RESOURCES

- **The Existential Therapy Center**

A resource dedicated to existential and thanatophobia-related therapy, exploring how to live meaningfully in the face of mortality. Visit Existential Therapy Center.

- **The Death Anxiety Handbook**

A practical guide by Robert Firestone on overcoming fear of death through psychological and existential frameworks. Available at Amazon.

- **The Center for Loss & Life Transition**

Led by Dr. Alan Wolfelt, this center provides grief and loss resources, including workshops and training. Learn ore at Center for Loss.

Chapter 16:

Additional Journaling Prompts An Invitation to Attune To Your Inner Simian

Congratulations, fellow ape, for swinging your way this far into the rainforest of self-discovery. You've climbed trees, observed the canopy, and perhaps even seen the forest for the trees. Every chapter, every reflection, has been an opportunity to reconnect with your inner simian energies—the primal wisdom that resides within us all. As you move forward, I encourage you to pause and ask yourself: What have I learned from the great apes that inhabit my own spirit? Are there ways I can embowwdy the calm strength of a gorilla, the curiosity of a chimp, the playful harmony of a bonobo, or the thoughtful independence of an orangutan? The rainforest is vast, tangled, and alive with possibility, but you've proven you can navigate it with courage, curiosity, and compassion.

As you continue your journey, take a moment to reflect on what you've discovered about yourself and how you see the world now. Have you found new ways to balance the demands of daily life with a deeper connection to the wildness within you? Do you feel more attuned to the rhythms of your instincts, your relationships, and the environment around you? These questions aren't meant to have final answers—they're your guideposts as you move forward. Remember, the rainforest doesn't reveal all its secrets at once, but each step brings you closer to its heart.

This book has been a tool—an imperfect, non-comprehensive first attempt to synthesize heaps of research, integrate oodles of psychedelic downloads from my guides, and further the critical conversation about what we, as a species, need to do next. It is not the final word, nor should it be. I welcome feedback and critique, but if we keep tossing the baby out with the bathwater—without recognizing how precious the baby is, how valuable the water is, how dangerous the act is, and how much love goes into simply doing our best—well, then, we're just going to keep repeating that cycle a while longer.

But I truly believe we can do better. We are doing better. And with your help, we'll continue along that path. More open hearts, more soulful actions—and who knows what we might evolve into?

History reminds us that progress is rarely neat, linear, or perfect. Take Dr. Marie Maynard Daly, for example. As a Black woman in science in the mid-20th century, she had every systemic barrier stacked against her. And yet, she pushed forward—earning a Ph.D. in chemistry in 1947 and going on to make groundbreaking discoveries about the link between high blood pressure and heart disease. Her research paved the way for life-saving treatments that continue to benefit millions today. She worked not with certainty, but with persistence, knowing that the answers would emerge through steady effort, curiosity, and resilience. I ain't no Dr. Daly, but I am determined to do some of these practices, simianly simple as some are, on the DAILY... and that is the world I shall live in til death do us part...

That's all any of us can do. Move forward with care. Hold space for uncertainty. Question the systems we're told to trust. Refine rather than reject. Because if we can meet the messiness of progress with curiosity rather than fear, we might just shape a world that is kinder, more just, and more whole than we ever imagined.

So, thank you—for reading, for thinking, for nudging the stone a little closer to the goal line. We are all in the same race, after all.

PRIMER PROMPTS FOR YOUR INNER PRIMATE

1. Seeing the Forest for the Trees:

- What lessons from the great apes resonate most with you?

- Are there moments in your life where you've prioritized the trees—small, immediate details— over the forest—the bigger picture? How can you balance the two?

2. Swinging Through Challenges:

- What is one area in your life where you feel stuck, like you're clinging to the same branch for too long?

- How might you channel the adaptability of a chimpanzee or the thoughtful problem-solving of an orangutan to navigate this challenge?

3. Tapping into Your Inner Bonobo:

- When was the last time you diffused tension with playfulness, affection, or humor?

- How can you bring more harmony and joy into your relationships—whether at work, at home, or in your community?

4. The Strength of the Gorilla Troop:

- Who are the members of your "troop"? These could be family, friends, or chosen community. How do you show loyalty and care for them?

- Is there someone in your life who might need a little extra protection or support right now? How can you offer that in a way that feels authentic to you?

5. Orangutan Wisdom:

- Reflect on your relationship with solitude. Do you make time for quiet reflection, or does the busyness of life crowd it out?

- What would it look like to create your own "nest" for rest and contemplation? How might this practice deepen your connection to yourself and your purpose?

As we swing toward the conclusion of our journey together, it's time to unleash your inner primate and embark on some additional self-discovery. Throughout this book, we've explored the concept of cognitive liberty—the freedom to own your thoughts and embrace change, free from societal constraints. Now, let's put that into action.

In a world that often demands conformity, protecting your cognitive liberty is a radical act of self-care and resistance. Our brains, much like a lush jungle canopy, thrive when given space to rest, recharge, and grow.

These prompts are designed to challenge your thinking, spark self-discovery, and help you swing toward a more liberated and resilient mindset.

To deepen your connection to the themes we've explored, your inner primate, and the wider world, consider these prompts as opportunities for further reflection. Remember, evolution isn't about perfection—it's about growth, exploration, and staying curious. Celebrate your progress, and feel free to navigate these prompts at your own pace.

So, grab your journal, voice memo, or any tool that helps you process these thoughts. Ready, set, go bananas!

Take your time, and know that nothing really is a waste of time, especially when we have Kindsight (compassionate hindsight) on our side

Chapter 1: Ape-solute Kindness

- Reflect on a time when you performed an act of kindness that felt truly transformative. What motivated you, and how did it affect you and the recipient?

- Identify one relationship in your life where cynicism or fear has created distance. What small act of kindness could you offer to rebuild trust or connection?

- Imagine kindness as a ripple in a pond. What larger societal impact could your personal acts of kindness create over time?

Chapter 2: Banana Peels of Failure

- Write about a recent failure and how it shaped your understanding of yourself. How might this experience be reframed as a stepping stone?

- Explore the concept of "playful failure." What's one area in your life where you could afford to take more risks and laugh at the outcomes?

- List three lessons you've learned from failure that you couldn't have gained from success. How can you use those lessons moving forward?

Chapter 3: Rewilding Your Inner Chimp

- Think of a time when you felt most connected to nature. What did it teach you about yourself and your place in the world?

- Describe one modern "cage" in your life—a habit, environment, or mindset that feels unnatural. How can you begin to break free?

- Imagine spending a day entirely "rewilded." What would you do, and how would it differ from your typical routine?

Chapter 4: Unlearning the Jungle Rules

- Identify one "rule" of society you've always followed without questioning. What would your life look like if you challenged or rewrote it?

- Reflect on a time when you went against societal norms. What resistance or freedom did you encounter?

- Write about a hierarchy or power structure you see in your community. How could it be redesigned to promote equality and collaboration?

Chapter 5: Radical Rest in the Canopy

- Describe your current relationship with rest. Is it guilt-free, or do you feel pressure to stay productive?

- Write about a time when taking intentional rest led to a breakthrough or new perspective.

- Imagine creating a "rest revolution" in your life. What changes would you make to prioritize stillness and recovery?

Chapter 6: Sacred Grooming

- Reflect on a daily habit or ritual you currently do. How could you infuse it with more intention and care?

- Write about a time when an act of care—giving or receiving—deepened a relationship.

- Explore the concept of "grooming" as connection. What's one way you could use everyday interactions to strengthen bonds with others?

Chapter 7: Chimpanzee-ing Playfulness

- Recall a moment when you felt completely playful and uninhibited. What allowed you to let go?

- Write about an area of your life where you've become too serious. How could you bring more playfulness into it?

- Imagine play as a form of healing. What playful activity could help you process a current challenge or emotion?

Chapter 8: Primate Picks: Conscious Consumption

- Analyze your media diet. How does what you consume affect your mindset, emotions, and actions?

- Reflect on a recent choice you made about food, entertainment, or another resource. How aligned was it with your values?

- Create a "conscious consumption" plan for the next week. What changes will you make, and why?

Chapter 9: Troop Mentality Over Me-First Thinking

- Write about a time when community support helped you overcome a challenge. What made that support effective?

- Reflect on an area of your life where you tend to prioritize individualism over collaboration. How might a troop mentality serve you better?

- Imagine building a stronger community in one aspect of your life. What steps would you take to foster connection and mutual support?

Chapter 10: Beating Your Chest for Justice

- Write about a cause or issue that stirs your passion. What bold action could you take to advocate for change?

- Reflect on a time when you spoke your truth, even though it was difficult. What did you learn from the experience?

- Imagine a world where everyone "beat their chest" for justice. What would that look like, and what role would you play?

Chapter 11: Love Your Own Fur First

- Reflect on a time when you compared yourself to others. What did it teach you about your own unique strengths?

- Write a love letter to yourself, celebrating your quirks, flaws, and individuality.

- Explore the concept of "radical self-love." What's one step you can take today to embrace your authentic self?

Chapter 12: Ape-reciating All Pronouns: Evolving Language as a Tool for Healing, Not Harm

- Reflect on a recent conversation where your words may have unintentionally objectified someone. How could you rephrase your language to honor their humanity?

- Consider a group you feel disconnected from. What labels or narratives have influenced this perception? How might changing your language about them alter your understanding?

- Observe your self-talk during moments of failure. How can you transform this inner dialogue to foster self-compassion and growth?

Chapter 13: Swinging Offline: Digital Detox for Primal Clarity

- Reflect on how technology shapes your daily life. What benefits does it bring, and what does it take away?

- Write about a time when you unplugged from screens. How did it affect your mood, focus, and connections?

- Create a digital detox plan for the next month. What boundaries will you set, and what's your goal?

Chapter 14: Reclaiming the Commons: Shared Spaces, Shared Futures

- Reflect on a shared space—physical or virtual—that has been meaningful to you. What made it special?

- Write about an issue affecting public resources or spaces in your community. How could you contribute to its solution?

- Imagine designing a shared space that fosters connection and collaboration. What would it look like, and how would it function?

Chapter 15: Where the Wild Things Mourn: Embracing the End

- Reflect on your relationship with mortality. How does the idea of impermanence shape the way you live?

- Write about a time when confronting death—your own or someone else's—gave you new clarity or purpose.

- Imagine writing a "life manifesto" inspired by the awareness of death. What guiding principles would you include?

As you engage with these prompts, remember: the goal isn't to "get it right." It's to stay curious, to question, and to keep growing. Share your reflections, insights, and questions with those in your "troop"—because together, we are stronger, wiser, and braver than we could ever be alone. Let your inner primate lead the way!

About the Author

Ken Breniman is a yoga therapist, LCSW, psychedelic integration specialist, and storyteller who believes in the power of subversive acts to transform humanity. With decades of experience helping individuals reconnect with their primal instincts and navigate life's challenges, Ken combines scientific insight, spiritual wisdom, and playful creativity in his work. His unique approach bridges the gap between ancient traditions and modern challenges, offering readers tools to live more authentically, compassionately, and courageously.

Ken's passion for fostering cognitive liberty and neuroplastic growth stems from his own life journey—a path filled with both failures and breakthroughs. A self-proclaimed "primate enthusiast," Ken draws inspiration from the animal kingdom to remind us that kindness, collaboration, and playfulness are not just human traits but universal truths. Through his work, Ken invites others to swing toward a future filled with connection, justice, and joy.

Postscript of Provocation

As I conclude this guide, I encourage you to choose your own path, just as I have chosen mine. During the lockdown—a term and experience we're all still processing—I devised a plan to maintain my sanity. I conspired with my inner child to embark on a pilgrimage I'd dreamed of since learning about the Great Apes. After saving for six months and dipping into my savings, my partner and I journeyed to Uganda to visit the chimpanzees in Kibale National Park and the mountain gorillas in Bwindi Impenetrable National Park.

Aware of Uganda's notorious stance on LGBTQ+ rights, we, two obviously gay men, approached the trip with caution. Staying in upscale ecolodges and accompanied by our dedicated tour guide, Africano, we toned down our exuberant expressions to respect local customs. Our focus was on the apes and those committed to their conservation. We brought two suitcases filled with N95 masks, courtesy of a U.S. nonprofit aiming to do more good than our country does harm. I also gifted the Conservation Through Public Health organization one of my cherished singing bowls, which, as the veterinarians later shared, they still use to begin and end meetings.

This journey wasn't just a means to stay sane during the pandemic; it also coincided with my 53rd birthday. On that day, we ventured into the lush Bwindi Impenetrable Forest, guided by a man who had dedicated his life to gorilla conservation long before Hollywood spotlighted Dian Fossey's story. As we walked, he pointed out the differences between the left and right sides of the path. To the left lay the old forest, teeming with the full cycle of life—growth, decay, and regeneration. To the right was a newer, younger rainforest, vibrant yet more penetrable.

He explained that the left side was once farmland, where human-ape conflicts were common. Farmers who chose to stay nearby agreed to cultivate tea plants, the one crop gorillas avoid, providing a sustainable solution that benefits both humans and apes. This innovative solution benefits both local communities and wildlife conservation. This revelation was a testament to the miracles that occur when we step back and allow nature to thrive.

Throughout our journey, we witnessed a remarkable baby boom among endangered species: young giraffes trotting beside their mothers, playful elephant calves, twin lion cubs learning to hunt, and an unforgettable baby gorilla tending to its mother's wounds. These experiences underscored a profound truth: when we step back and allow nature to thrive, miracles unfold.

Was it worth the time and money to visit Uganda and spend my 53rd birthday in the Honeymoon Suite at a fancy ecolodge during a pandemic? Absolutely.

Do I believe in the power of individual and collective subversive acts? Without a doubt.

I've done what I set out to do, and while this guide may be incomplete and the journey ahead daunting, I've given my best. That's all any of us can hope for.

And, as a parting message, I offer you this..one last invitation to see what is really up with that inner Ape you have cared for all these years.

If you're willing to engage in one final act of subversive play, I invite you to approach a mirror—whether you choose to sit, stand, or even lie beside it. You don't have to look directly into it; just being near, with eyes open or closed, acknowledges your presence. Even if this is the first time you've embraced this exercise throughout our journey together, that's perfectly okay. After all, this may be my first attempt at crafting a survival manual, and I fully admit I so seldom do 'everything' a self-help book invites me to do.

So, I dare you to give a playful side-eye to your reflection or to this book—either way, you're participating! This is a gentle nudge to engage in a moment of self-recognition. Remember, our primate cousins have their own ways of interacting with mirrors, and so do you. Just be cautious not to slip on any metaphorical banana peels as you venture back into your own personal jungle, town, city, or village. The world is waiting for your unique contribution.

While the "Planet of the Apes" franchise may have sequels in the works, all I can offer is a hint that more learning adventures await if you're inclined to join me again. Thank you for embarking on this journey with me; it's been a wild ride, and I look forward to the possibility of more shared explorations in the future.

As the Muppets sang at the end of their original movie, "Life's like a movie, write your own ending." I've done what I came here to do. This survival guide, though imperfect and daunting, represents my best effort. That's all any of us can offer.

Thank you for journeying from nightmare to hope with me. I invite you to join the lovers and dreamers in seeking the wonders within us and, someday, all around us.

Cited Sources & Bibliography

- *ABC News. (2016, May 30). Gorilla carries 3-year-old boy to safety in 1996 incident.*

- *Anderson, J. R., et al. (2010). Chimpanzee deaths and the grieving process. American Journal of Primatology.*

- *Ardrey, R. (1967). African Genesis: A Personal Investigation into the Animal Origins and Nature of Man. Dell Publishing.*

- *Bekoff, M. (2001). Social play behavior: Cooperation, fairness, trust, and the evolution of morality.*

- *Boesch, C. (2001). Cooperative hunting roles among wild chimpanzees. Human Nature.*

- *Brown, B. (2012). Daring Greatly: How the Courage to Be Vulnerable Transforms the Way We Live, Love, Parent, and Lead.*

- *Brown, S. (2009). Play: How It Shapes the Brain, Opens the Imagination, and Invigorates the Soul.*

- *Buber, M. (1923). I and Thou. Charles Scribner's Sons.*

- *Cacioppo, J. T., et al. (2014). Social neuroscience: How a lack of connection affects our brains and bodies.*

- *Center for Compassion and Altruism Research and Education. (2019). The science of growth mindset.*

- *Cigna. (2020). Loneliness in America report.*

- *De Waal, F. B. M. (1982). Chimpanzee Politics: Power and Sex Among Apes.*

- *De Waal, F. B. M. (1997). Bonobo: The Forgotten Ape.*

- *De Waal, F. B. M. (2005). Our Inner Ape: A Leading Primatologist Explains Why We Are Who We Are. Riverhead Books.*

- *De Waal, F. (2009). The Age of Empathy: Nature's Lessons for a Kinder Society. Crown.*

- *Dinsmore-Tuli, U., & Dinsmore-Tuli, N. (n.d.). Yoga Nidra Network. Retrieved February 23, 2025, from https://www.yoganidranetwork.org/*

- *DiAngelo, R. (2018). White Fragility: Why It's So Hard for White People to Talk About Racism. Beacon Press.*

- *Dweck, C. S. (2006). Mindset: The New Psychology of Success.*

- *Elwert, F., & Christakis, N. A. (2008). The effect of widowhood on mortality by the causes of death of both spouses. American Journal of Public Health, 98(11), 2092–2098.*

- *Fargeat, C. (Director). (2024). The Substance [Film]. Working Title Films; Blacksmith.*

- *Field, T. (2010). Touch for socioemotional and physical well-being: A review.*

- *Fossey, D. (1983). Gorillas in the Mist.*

- *Fothergill, A., & Linfield, M. (Directors). (2012). Chimpanzee [Film]. Disneynature*

- *Franken, A. (1992). I'm good enough, I'm smart enough, and doggone it, people like me!: Daily affirmations by Stuart Smalley. Dell Publishing.*

- *Fredrickson, B. L. (2001). The role of positive emotions in positive psychology: The broaden-and-build theory of positive emotions.*

- *Ginsburg, R. B. (1996). My Own Words.*

- *Goleman, D. (2006). Social Intelligence: The New Science of Human Relationships. Bantam.*

- *Goodall, J. (1971). In the Shadow of Man. Houghton Mifflin.*

- *Goodall, J. (1986). The Chimpanzees of Gombe: Patterns of Behavior.*

- *Graeber, D., & Wengrow, D. (2021). The Dawn of Everything: A New History of Humanity. Farrar, Straus and Giroux.*

- *Hanazuka, Y., Shimizu, M., Takaoka, H., & Midorikawa, A. (2018). Orangutans (Pongo pygmaeus) recognize their own past actions. Royal Society Open Science, 5(12), 181497.*

- *Hare, B. (2020). Survival of the Friendliest.*

- *Harari, Y. N. (2015). Sapiens: A Brief History of Humankind. Harper.*

- *Hertenstein, M. J., & Weiss, S. J. (2011). The communication of emotion via touch.*

- *Holt-Lunstad, J. (2015). Loneliness and social isolation as risk factors for mortality: A meta-analytic review.*

- *Hrdy, S. B. (2009). Mothers and Others: The Evolutionary Origins of Mutual Understanding. Harvard University Press.*

- *Huberman, A. (Host). (2025, August 15). Dr. Martha Beck: Accessing your best self with mind-body practices, belief testing & imagination [Audio podcast episode]. In Huberman Lab. Huberman Lab.*

- *Human Rights Campaign. (2023). State of equality report.*

- *Huxley, A. (1932). Brave new world. Chatto & Windus.*

- *Jenkinson, S. (2015). Die Wise: A Manifesto for Sanity and Soul. North Atlantic Books.*

- *Kaba, M. (2021). We Do This 'Til We Free Us: Abolitionist Organizing and Transforming Justice. Haymarket Books.*

- *Kimmerer, R. W. (2013). Braiding Sweetgrass: Indigenous Wisdom, Scientific Knowledge, and the Teachings of Plants. Milkweed Editions.*

- *Klar, M., & Kasser, T. (2009). Some benefits of being an activist: Measuring activism and its role in psychological well-being. Political Psychology.*

- *Kotis, G. (Writer), & Hollmann, M. (Composer & Lyricist). (2001). Urinetown: The Musical [Stage production]. Directed by J. Rando.*

- *Lakoff, G., & Johnson, M. (1980). Metaphors We Live By. University of Chicago Press.*

- *Lannen, P. K., Wolfe, J., Prigerson, H. G., Onelov, E., & Kreicbergs, U. C. (2008). Unresolved grief in a national sample of bereaved parents: Impaired mental and physical health 4 to 9 years later. Journal of Clinical Oncology, 26(36), 5870–5876.*

- *Levine, P. A. (1997). Waking the Tiger: Healing Trauma. North Atlantic Books.*

- *Lonsdorf, E. V., et al. (2021). Tool use in captive and wild gorillas: Insights into intentionality. Primate Cognition Studies Journal.*

- *Loudenback,T. (2024))A list of companies that have pulled back on DEI, including Amazon, Google, Walmart, and Meta." Business Insider.*

- *Macy, J., & Brown, M. (2014). Coming Back to Life: The Updated Guide to the Work That Reconnects. New Society Publishers.*

- *Mallapur, A. (2005). The effect of captivity on behavior in primates. Applied Animal Behaviour Science.*

- *Mill, J. S. (1859). On liberty. J. W. Parker and Son.*

- *Miller, R. (2010). Yoga Nidra: A Meditative Practice for Deep Relaxation and Healing. Sounds True.*

- *Neff, K. (2011). Self-compassion: The proven power of being kind to yourself. William Morrow.*

- *Niemöller, M. (1946). First they came.*

- *Onderstijn, M. (Director). (2012). The Life of Death [Film]. Retrieved from https://youtu.be/ofnCdC8P70g*

- *Orwell, G. (1949). 1984. Secker & Warburg.*

- *Ostrom, E. (1990). Governing the Commons: The Evolution of Institutions for Collective Action.*

- *Plevin, J. (2019). The healing magic of forest bathing: Finding calm, creativity, and connection in the natural world. Ten Speed Press.*

- *Project for Public Spaces. (n.d.). What is placemaking? Available at: pps.org.*

- *Rosenberg, M. B. (2003). Nonviolent Communication: A Language of Life. PuddleDancer Press.*

- *Ross, S. R., & Lukas, K. E. (2006). Differences in behavior of captive and wild primates. American Journal of Primatology.*

- *Sapolsky, R. M. (2017). Behave: The Biology of Humans at Our Best and Worst. Penguin Press.*

- *Shear, M. K., Ghesquiere, A., & Glickman, K. (2013). Bereavement and complicated grief. Current Psychiatry Reports, 15(11), 406.*

- *Singer, T., & Klimecki, O. M. (2014). Empathy and compassion.*

- *Stroebe, M., Schut, H., & Stroebe, W. (2007). Health outcomes of bereavement. The Lancet, 370(9603), 1960–1973.*

- *Tattersall, I. (2012). Masters of the Planet: The Search for Our Human Origins. Palgrave Macmillan.*

- *The Trevor Project. (2023). National survey on LGBTQ+ mental health.*

- *Thich Nhat Hanh. (1997). The Heart of the Buddha's Teaching. Parallax Press.*

- *Thich Nhat Hanh. (2002). No Death, No Fear.*

- *Varoufakis, Y. (2024). Technofeudalism: What killed capitalism. Melville House.*